5 RULES TO IMPROVE YOUR CONVERSATIONS

HOW TO FIND YOUR VOICE, COMMUNICATE WITH
EMPATHY TO RESOLVE CONFLICTS, AND IMPROVE
RELATIONSHIPS AT WORK, HOME, OR ANYWHERE

SOCIAL IQ ACADEMY

CONTENTS

Introduction   v

1. Do Your Words Matter?   1
Understanding The Four Tenets Of Mindful Communication

2. Rule #1: Speak Your True Self With
Mindful Communication   17
*Finding And Using Your Authentic Expression When
Communicating*

3. Rule #2: Use The Power Of Self-
Awareness   40
*How Self-Reflection Helps You Manage Emotions And
Biases When Communicating*

4. Rule #3: Don't Just Hear—But Listen!   60
*How Going From Hearing To Understanding Transforms
The Conversations You Make*

5. Rule #4: All About Empathy And Cultural
Intelligence   80
*How Being Proficient In These Concepts Can Help You
Communicate Better*

6. Rule #5: Don't Be Afraid To Face
Conflicts!   95
*How To Kill Conflicts With Kindness… And Good
Communication Skills!*

7. Why Talking To Yourself Is NOT A Bad
Thing   119
*How Inward Dialogues Prepare You For Outward
Conversations*

8. Nurturing Relationships IRL   139
*How To Speak Better To Build Up Relationships With Your
Inner Circle, Instead Of Tearing Them Down*

9. Let's Make It Work At Work!   165
*Crack The Secrets To Being A Master Communicator In The
Workplace*

10. Turn Strangers Into Meaningful
Connections   196
How To Overcome Initial Hesitations, Build Your
Confidence, And Speak Well With People Outside Your Circle

11. The Talk That Changes The World   218
How To Use Your Voice To Uplift Others And Be A Force
Of Positive Change

Afterword   239
References   243
Disclaimer   257

INTRODUCTION

From the moment of birth, communication begins. The cry of a baby is so powerful for this purpose that our heart rate and blood pressure increase, even when it is not our own child![1] Communicating is an essential human activity. It's the way we share our feelings and thoughts. It's how we let others know our needs and how we want to have those met. It's the way we learn about these feelings, thoughts, and needs in others. Most importantly, it's how we connect and belong.

We all have interactions with many different types of people, some from our same background and others from diverse cultures. Whether it's for getting along better with your family and friends, being a part of a well-functioning work team, or advocating for social change, this book will help you on the path to rich and meaningful relationships and experiences. I look forward to sharing this through the lens of my years of experience as a psychologist and life coach helping others improve their communication and thereby improve their relationships.

This book builds on mindfulness, but it is not about disengaging from the world or letting yourself only be guided by intuition rather than conscious effort. For example, I might offer meditation as a strategy for calming emotions and turning inward for self-discovery, but only occasionally. Rather, you will find many strategies that match the topic at hand. On the topics, we will look at their research-basis. Having both conducted research and being immersed in it, I will frame the topics within examples and scenarios. You'll have activities and exercises to implement and resources to continue your journey. That's important because improving conversations will be an ongoing task in life.

Communicating effectively takes time, effort, patience, and commitment. When it goes well, it is rewarding and fulfilling. When it goes poorly, we can feel upset and lonely. In *5 Rules To Improve Your Conversations: How to find your voice, communicate with empathy to resolve conflicts and improve relationships at work, home, or anywhere*, we will take a journey through communicating to achieve these goals.

We will cover communication in all the settings where we have conversations with others. You will learn the underlying concepts, why knowing yourself and finding your voice matters, and effective and powerful strategies to establish and maintain positive and fulfilling relationships. Lastly, we've sprinkled some of the rules, as sort of tips, to help you improve your communication skills.

The theme that runs through this book is mindful communication. This interaction style means being fully present in the moment, nonjudgmental, not overreacting, expressing empathy, and being authentic and genuine. It's a powerful approach to decrease misunderstandings and increase mutual respect.

In short, this book is designed to teach, motivate, and inspire you to achieve the biggest return on your communication investment. It can be a tall order for anyone, but we break it all down for you. We begin with the core principles of peaceful communication. Then we move to self-awareness and the role you play as the central actor in conversations. Knowing yourself and how to manage your emotions through introspection and self-awareness is a key part of mindful communication.

We will take a deep dive into why misunderstandings and conflict occur and how you can resolve these with empathy and respect. In particular, active listening is a technique you will learn that will serve you well in any situation and you will see step-by-step how to apply it.

Having both practiced and written in this area, I've seen firsthand the importance of communication and relationships. Many people struggle in this area—some because they are aware they have weaknesses, others because they think they know how to communicate well, but are missing key steps and skills. The good news is that with an open mind and willingness, they do improve their communications and the strength and health of their relationships…and so can you. I'm excited to be your guide as you embark on this journey to improve your conversations!

Are you ready to reap the benefits? Keep reading to first learn about the principles of nonviolent communication.

Lilla Dale McManis, MEd, PhD

1

DO YOUR WORDS MATTER?

UNDERSTANDING THE FOUR TENETS OF MINDFUL COMMUNICATION

People have told Kevin to 'chill out' or 'calm down' for as long as he can remember. He will admit he's got strong opinions and can get insistent on sharing them. He knows when he does this, he comes across as dominating and kind of a know-it-all. Sometimes, he gets into pretty heated arguments with people.

Recently he saw an ad for an app for mindfulness and thought, "Why not?" He's been slowly realizing that he needs to do something proactive to improve his situation. He's hoping the app will help him be more calm since that's what people tell him he needs to do. He's been using the app for a few weeks, and he thinks he feels calmer inside.

He's confused, though, because he went to dinner with his cousin who was in town last weekend. When Kevin saw the high prices on the menu, he started sharing his opinion on inflation. He was trying to stay calm, but his cousin was really pushing his buttons and making it worse because he kept telling Kevin to relax.

When they left the restaurant, his cousin said, "Well, thanks for ruining dinner, dude. I never even got a chance to tell you how it feels now that I'm a new dad. It's pretty clear, though, that you don't care." Now, Kevin is discouraged and he's deleted the mindfulness app from his phone.

The term mindfulness seems to be everywhere you turn. Mindfulness, in popular media, can come across as a panacea for overall well-being. It commonly revolves around decreasing stress and increasing self-awareness. Practices like meditation and yoga are frequently suggested to achieve mindfulness. There is also a large community of researchers working in this space.

From academic journals to popular media to apps to sayings on T-shirts, mindfulness is easily one of those concepts that has captured the attention of all of us.

Figure 1.1 An overwhelmed woman looking over a stack of books[1]

Yet, just as we saw with Kevin, it is possible to be mindful and ineffective in communicating with others. Why?

Mindful communication is like a seesaw. On one side is mindfulness, being fully present and engaged in the moment in whatever you are doing. On the other is communication skills, the ability to express yourself effectively and comprehend and understand what others are saying and feeling.

If mindfulness and communication skills are balanced and working well together, everyone has a positive interaction. Otherwise, one person is stuck on the ground, and the other is hanging in the air. Neither can enjoy the experience!

There are scores of authors writing about what constitutes mindfulness, but let's take a look at the one put forward by Baer and her co-authors. In their definition, mindfulness calls upon us to give complete attention to what is being experienced in the current moment and doing so in a nonjudgmental and accepting way.

These researchers used a large number of measures and found that mindfulness comprises five components:

- Acting with awareness
- Observing
- Nonjudging
- Nonreacting
- Describing[2]

Importantly, these are not completely distinct from one another. Further, they interact with and influence one another. It's like they're 'playing in the same sandbox,' and what they create varies depending on how skilled the builders are!

Similarly, when it comes to communication, there are a multitude of ways to define this concept. Whole theories have emerged to try to do so. In fact, in the book *Theories of Human Communication*, Littlejohn and Foss contend that it's almost too difficult![3]

That said, it is important to have a way to define communication for our purposes. The one put forth by Adler and associates is widely accepted and easily understood. At its most basic level, when messages are exchanged between a sender and a receiver, this is communication.[4] Much like mindfulness, the communication process involves many facets, and it is dynamic. It also matters that the two people in the exchange have a shared understanding as they engage in communication. This applies to all relationships, whether they be personal, professional, or public.

Mindful communication takes communication further as an interaction style with several components. These are being self-aware by being fully present in the moment, not judging, not overreacting, expressing empathy, and being authentic and genuine. The underlying goal of mindful communication is to build healthy connections with others that result in a decrease in misunderstandings and an increase in mutual respect.[5]

Now, we can just start to see how mindfulness and communication can come together as a powerful game-changer for you.

Figure 1.2 Mastering the game of mindfulness and communication can be as easy as tic tac toe.[6]

In this book, we will be fully exploring the many aspects of mindful communication. But here in Chapter 1, we begin laying the groundwork for how mindful communication works. You will learn about the core principles and values. As we go through these, we'll take a deep dive into the importance of the three pillars of empathy, respect, and trust in relationships. We will look at the ways they interweave within nonviolent communication.

When you see the term 'nonviolent communication,' your first thought might be, "This doesn't apply to me. I don't hit anyone or throw things! Nobody does that to me, either!"

But have you ever encountered judgment, verbal demands, or disrespect—giving or receiving? If you're like most, then you have indeed experienced traditional communication. Nonviolent communication is the opposite. Here, interactions involve mutual choice and are more respectful and peaceful.

One of the most helpful ways to understand mindful communication is through the knowledge and application of nonviolent communication. Working as an international mediator, psychologist, and educator, Dr. Marshall Rosenberg developed the approach of Nonviolent Communication (NVC).[7]

Beginning in the 1960s, NVC became a worldwide phenomenon. It encompasses academic research as well as application through workshops, books, videos, and more.

This approach involves applying four core principles: observation, feelings, needs, and requests.

Core Principle 1: Observation

The first principle means observing without evaluating. We must learn to clearly say what is happening in a situation without adding judgment or interpretation. This step focuses on concrete, specific, and observable behaviors rather than vague or abstract evaluations.

When we observe without evaluating, we can communicate more effectively and build more authentic and understanding relationships with others.

Core Principle Two: Feelings

The second principle is identifying and expressing feelings. Here, we both connect with and express our emotions through self-awareness. We recognize that our feelings follow our needs, which are either being met or not being met. Our feelings need to be directly related to what is being observed by us and in an objective way.

Our ability to connect with others is enhanced when our feelings are expressed constructively. It does not matter the other person's culture or background. When we express our feelings in this way, we are able to develop relationships that are more meaningful.

Core Principle Three: Needs

Principle three of nonviolent communication is to identify the underlying needs behind our feelings.

It involves recognizing the universal human needs that are driving our emotions, such as safety, connection, autonomy (meaning choice and independence), and respect. We have feelings about our needs and these are highly interwoven with our individual and personal desires and values.

Through self-awareness, we can develop a higher degree of empathy and understanding in relationships by identifying and acknowledging that our human needs are a motivating force for the emotions we experience. This puts us on a path to having connections with others that are more fulfilling.

Core Principle Four: Requests

The fourth principle involves making clear, concrete, and actionable requests to meet our needs. It can be tempting to make demands and try to manipulate others to get our needs met. Yet, enriching our existence is possible by requesting specific and fair actions from others.

Dialogue that is empathetic and understanding is possible with requests made by us that are clear, concrete, and action-oriented. Relationships that are filled with more harmony and which are more fulfilling will now have a chance to flourish.

The Pillars Of Nonviolent Communication

To apply the principles of nonviolent communication, it is helpful to know that this approach is built on three main pillars. These are *empathy, respect, and trust in relationships*. These pillars are part of how change happens through NVC. Our perspectives shift on how we think about other people. This goes beyond just learning communication skills.[8]

Jenny and her boyfriend Alonzo are at a football game, and he seems upset. Alonzo is usually very upbeat, but today, he's been uncharacteristically quiet.

At halftime, Jenny and Alonzo make their way to the concession stand. Jenny decides to ask him if everything is okay. He steps away from the rushing crowd, stops, and seems hesitant. Jenny waits to see what he's going to say. Finally, he says he's upset about the way she treats him like a child.

At first, Jenny is shocked. In her mind, she and Alonzo are the perfect couple. Jenny has to catch herself because she almost says this aloud.

Instead, Jenny actively empathizes with Alonzo. After all, she's felt this way herself in past relationships.

Jenny acknowledges Alonzo's feelings: "I'm sorry to hear that. It must be really tough for you when I come across that way." She tells Alonzo she knows there needs to be many and much deeper conversations and she is open to that because her relationship with him is very important to her.

Alonzo looks Jenny in the eyes and says, "Thank you, Jenny. I was worried about how you'd react if I told you how I was feeling. Knowing our relationship means you're willing to work things out with me gives me a lot of hope.

We have all likely come across the term empathy. At its heart, empathy is the capacity to understand and share the feelings experienced by another person. You can put yourself in someone else's shoes and understand their thoughts, emotions, and their unique point of view. This is essential for building strong relationships. It is part of the backbone of communicating effectively and nonviolently.

Nonviolent communication is a powerful tool for building empathy and resolving conflict.[9][10] Koopman and Seliga reviewed impact studies and found the NVC model had a positive effect on building empathy. This allowed individuals to increase their understanding of others and brought out their compassion. People also didn't shy away from conflict. Instead, they saw empathy as a tool to resolve differences successfully.[10]

Once you empathetically gain insight into someone's perspective and what matters and motivates them, a solid foundation for resolving conflict is built. De-escalating the situation is more probable when people can connect across their differences. Finding win-win solutions is much more likely when 'protecting your corner' isn't top of mind.

Another essential pillar is respect. In NVC, respect is about valuing each person's needs and feelings without judgment or criticism. It means listening with genuine empathy and understanding, even when you disagree with them. In NVC, respect also involves honesty and authenticity during communication, all while being attentive to the impact of your words on others.

The people you communicate with most regularly are likely those with whom you are the closest. Frei and Shaver wanted to study the attributes that people associate with feelings of respect in a variety of close relationships. They found that having and showing respect is about being trustworthy, considerate, and accepting.

What is very encouraging? Respect begets respect! It's like a mutual cycle. Further, when the two people in a relationship communicate respectfully, not only does their respect grow, but so does their trust in one another. And a bonus? You will like each other more.[11]

Trust in relationships is the third pillar of NVC. Psychologist Jeffry Simpson studies close relationships and interpersonal processes from different theoretical perspectives. His comprehensive review of the foundations of interpersonal trust highlights that it is one of the most essential and desired goals of human beings. Without it, relationships simply cannot be healthy and secure.[12]

Why? If you don't feel you are in a safe space for communication, you are less likely to be open and honest. After all, nobody wants to feel attacked.

Applying NVC establishes a compassionate connection that allows both you and the other person to get your needs met. To fully connect, you must feel you can trust someone enough to be vulnerable and share what you truly need.

Figure 1.3 Two women holding hands and connecting with each other.[13]

Action Steps

We've now seen how important empathy, respect, and trust in relationships are for peaceful, effective, and satisfying communication. Let's look at these interwoven and in action within the four core principles.

How To Practice Observation

Look and listen objectively. Pay attention to the behaviors that can clearly be observed. Describe them, but leave out judgments. This reduces misunderstandings.

> Instead of saying, "You're always running late!"
> Try saying, "I notice you're frequently not on time."

How To Practice Feelings

Express feelings without placing blame, either on yourself or others. However, taking responsibility is important. Empathy and true connection can then flourish.

> Rather than saying, "I get ticked off when you're late!"
> Try saying, "Being on time is important to me, so I feel frustrated when I have to wait."

How To Practice Needs

Everyone has needs. Identify these. Think about them. Put them into words to express what matters to you. Encourage the same for others. Through understanding what is underneath emotions and behaviors, you can collaborate to meet everyone's needs.

> Rather than saying, "You never put me first!"
> Try saying, "I want to feel I'm a priority to you."

How To Practice Requests

Frame requests positively and respectfully. Make them clear and specific. Include the action desired. Most importantly, this principle focuses on cooperation and building goodwill.

> Instead of saying, "Take the trash out right now!"
> Try saying, "Would you be willing to take the trash out before I start cooking?"

Chapter Summary

Mindful communication has the potential to be life-changing for you. It can positively transform interactions. Rather than being in an endless cycle of misunderstanding, confusion, and ultimately alienation, like Kevin experiences, mindful communication allows compassionate and empathetic communication where relationships can grow healthy and deep like the one Jenny and Alonzo are well on their way to experiencing.

The key takeaways for you from this chapter are:

- You can practice mindfulness yet still be an ineffective communicator. When this happens, neither you nor your partner in the interaction will get your needs met.
- Combining mindfulness with the principles of nonviolent communication, on the other hand, allows you and the other person to feel safe through empathy, compassion, respect, and sensitivity. Doing so builds relationships that can be strong, lasting, and fulfilling.
- Learning how to engage in mindful and nonviolent communication takes work and practice. The most challenging aspect may be self-awareness. It can make us feel vulnerable to accept that we may be part of our problem.
- The good news is that nonviolent communication is achievable by understanding

and practicing the core principles of observation, feelings, needs, and requests.

In the next chapter, we will continue the journey and focus on mindful expression. We will talk about the significance of being more present, attentive, and mindful in conversations. We will also share the challenges because they do exist. I will share concrete techniques you can use to be more mindful, and to respectfully, but assertively, ensure your needs are met.

2

RULE #1: SPEAK YOUR TRUE SELF WITH MINDFUL COMMUNICATION
FINDING AND USING YOUR AUTHENTIC EXPRESSION WHEN COMMUNICATING

"Why can't you do anything right?!"

I think we can all relate to hearing some form of this statement. And we can all likely agree it is hurtful. Perhaps we have said this ourselves to someone and not realized just how much it can damage them.

- Your child, who spills at the table.
- Your boss when you make a mistake at work.
- Your parents when you make a poor financial decision.
- Your partner, who has a fender bender.

This list could go on into infinity!

Human beings often just blurt out without thinking. We may not intend to be harsh, critical, and judgmental. We don't think the other person is completely incompetent.

We certainly aren't expecting to damage how they feel about themselves. Yet this is what happens.

In a nutshell, this kind of communication is not thoughtful. It is not intentional. On the other hand, mindful expression *is* intentional. But as discussed in the previous chapter, it goes beyond being aware or mindful.

Mindful communication refers to expressing thoughts, feelings, and needs in a considerate manner. It involves being aware of the impact your words have on yourself and others. It means choosing your words carefully to convey your message effectively, all while preserving respect and empathy.

In nonviolent communication (NVC), expressing yourself through mindful communication is a key component. In this chapter, we will emphasize how NVC differs from conventional communication. We will see 'why' and 'how' to use mindful expression to promote authentic, peaceful connections with others by:

- Being aware of one's thoughts, feelings, and needs
- Expressing oneself honestly and clearly
- Communicating without blaming or criticizing others
- Expressing one's needs in a way that is assertive yet empathetic

The Power Of Mindful Communication

"I just had a great conversation!"

When we get the chance to experience this, we can't wait to tell others. It's almost like we've had an unexpected sighting of a rare creature in nature!

This feeling of elation and satisfaction is important for our emotional well-being. We may not really know why we feel so happy or label a certain interaction as 'great.' If asked, we may say things like, "She was a good listener," "They seemed to really know where I was coming from," or "I felt like I could tell him my secrets, and he wouldn't think I was a bad person."

What these people have in common is they are skilled at mindful communication. The good news is that you can be, too!

So, we've come to the first rule to improve your conversations: Practice mindful communication.

When mindful communication happens, not only will you see the benefits, but so will the people with whom you communicate. As Dr. Susanne Jones, current editor of the peer-reviewed psychology journal *Mindful* and a communication researcher and professor, writes that mindful expression is supportive. It helps us all cope with emotions we find challenging. It helps us be more willing to engage in situations we find aversive and to come out strong. This approach sends out signals of care, empathy, and encouragement within ourselves and to others. These are also hallmarks of nonviolent communication.[1]

The Role Of Mindfulness

Mindful expression has a wide range of benefits, and a key mechanism is the practice of mindfulness. Research into mindfulness training has been found to reduce worry, anxiety, depression, and anger. How? It helps us regulate our internal thoughts and emotions.[2]

When we can stop our mind from racing, stop the chatter, stop the what-ifs, and so on, we can have deeper and clearer insight into how we tend to think. If we reach this stage, we will have a chance to break old negative thinking habits and create positive ones.

This more thoughtful, curated, and positive mindset allows us to go into interactions and express ourselves mindfully. Now we have more tools to strengthen our relationships, resolve and heal conflicts, have our needs met, and reach our goals.

Practicing Mindfulness

Before we dive into how to practice and achieve mindfulness, let's talk about what mindfulness is not and what it is. It's not about 'emptying the mind.' Rather, mindfulness is being fully present in the moment. It is being purposeful about observing your thoughts and doing so without judging.

It's not about finding a way to 'escape reality.' Rather than avoiding uncomfortable emotions or situations, mindfulness means being open to acknowledging and accepting that you are experiencing these challenges. This process can bring up feelings of vulnerability but it can help to remember that it is necessary for growth.

Finally, mindfulness is not a 'quick fix.' It takes time, consistent practice, and sometimes emotional pain to achieve the state of mindfulness. Similarly, it takes patience to see the benefits—while they are substantial, they are gradual.

With this foundation in mind, here are several ways to develop mindfulness.

Meditation

Meditation is recommended by practitioners and scholars alike as a key practice to achieve mindfulness. According to the US National Institutes of Health, "The term 'meditation' refers to a variety of practices that focus on mind and body integration and are used to calm the mind and enhance overall well-being."[3]

Meditation is a core mindfulness practice that involves getting comfortable, usually seated. You then focus your attention on something specific and tangible. This could be an object, your breath, a mantra, or the sensations you feel in your body.

Here is how that might look:

Joan is dreading the upcoming visit this afternoon with her parents. Her mom is getting a bit hard of hearing, and Joan has to speak louder than usual. This triggers Joan's memories of shouting at her mother when she was a teenager. It brings her back to those difficult times and she feels guilty about how she behaved.

On top of that, her dad takes every opportunity to tell Joan how irresponsible it is that her son wants to take a gap year between high school and college. She has started questioning whether she should be supporting this. She's been feeling very anxious recently about whether this is a good idea and it is causing her relationship with her son to be strained.

As all these emotions flood through Joan, her heart starts to race, and she feels slightly nauseous. She knows she needs to find her inner calm before leaving the house. She decides to sit comfortably on her couch. She closes her eyes and breathes in deeply. Joan can feel the tension in her body start to dissipate. She focuses on her breath, noting how it feels as she inhales and exhales.

As thoughts drift into her mind, Joan acknowledges them without judgment. She gently brings her focus back to her breath. She experiences a sense of calmness and relaxation. After a few minutes, she opens her eyes and stretches.

Joan feels refreshed and centered. She carries this sense of peace with her as she visits with her parents, feeling calmer and more collected as they chat.

There are many meditation practices and tools, such as courses, books, and apps to explore, to discover which will work well for you.

<u>Journaling</u>

Putting your thoughts and emotions into words through journaling or expressive writing can facilitate mindfulness. It encourages reflection so that you are more aware of your inner world. Often, in doing so, you will get clarity and more understanding. This can reduce your feelings of uneasiness and allow you to have those 'ah ha' moments!

Here are some tips on how to get the most out of journaling for mindfulness:

1. Make journaling a habit by choosing a time and place to write without distraction. You may have to try a few places and times before you find what works best. Don't be shy either about telling others this is a time when you need to be undisturbed.
2. As you start your journaling session, try to have an overarching purpose. Perhaps you want to reflect on your feelings about something particular, to express what you are grateful for, or your dreams for the future. Some people find using a guided journal with topics, questions, and prompts helpful.
3. When writing, keep the overarching goals of mindfulness front and center. Be present in the moment; don't work to change how you are

feeling rather quiet the inclination to be critical and be compassionate toward yourself.

4. As you finish journaling, take time for reflection. What insights or patterns came to light? How can you apply what emerged going forward?

Connecting With Nature

'Getting some fresh air' is something most of us have either said or experienced someone else saying. There is a good reason for this. Research shows the physical and mental benefits of connecting with nature. Further, mindfulness mediates the relationship—meaning the process or pathway through which one influences the other.[4]

To help you practice this technique, here is how connecting with nature for mindfulness might look:

Brad had a lousy week at work. He got into a heated argument with a new co-worker and it really rattled him. It's Saturday morning and while he's tempted to stay inside and watch TV, he decides to take a walk on a nearby nature trail with his dog.

As he enters the forest, he immediately feels the peacefulness and beauty. He smiles to see how excited his pup is to be outside. As she tugs on the leash, Brad picks up his pace and in a few moments they reach a clearing with a stream. Brad begins to walk slowly. He hears the gentle rustling of leaves in the breeze, the chirping of birds overhead, and the gurgle of the stream.

He sits on a rock and watches the ripples dance across the water. His dog contentedly stretches out, snuggles next to him, and closes her eyes. Brad, too, closes his eyes and listens to the sounds around him. A feeling of calmness and inner peace comes over him. He gets a flash of insight and realizes that he has control of his emotions and can repair the damage with his co-worker.

After a while, he makes his way back to the start of the trail. He feels more centered. On the drive home, he realizes and accepts that some weeks are going to be challenging but he can always return to nature to practice mindfulness.

Figure 2.1 A man walking his dog at the nature park.[5]

There are many other ways to practice mindfulness, but these are some that are accessible to all of us. You may notice there are similar elements that run through them all. Becoming quiet, being open to the experience, and doing so without putting too much pressure on yourself, are all important to reaping the benefits of mindfulness techniques. To get more ideas, you can visit websites like Mindful.

Embracing vulnerability is a pathway to connection. Being vulnerable is crucial for healthy connections with others. So far, we have made sure to focus on first being vulnerable with ourselves as we practice self-awareness. Now let's take a look at understanding vulnerability with others and its relevance to communication and relationships.

Have you ever been on the verge of sharing something about yourself with someone and then pulled back? Why do you think this happened? What were you afraid of? What was the impact of not sharing on the relationship?

Similarly, have you gone ahead and shared? Was it a positive experience? Was it negative? What made the difference?

When you are willing to genuinely express what you are thinking, feeling, and needing, it can be intimidating. You open yourself up to the possibility of being rejected, misunderstood, or getting your feelings hurt. Yet, being honest and authentic, sharing your fears, insecurities, and weaknesses with others is where you can forge deep emotional and intimate bonds, as Khalifan and Barry affirm in their paper, "Vulnerable Disclosures and Partner Responding."[6]

As we have done previously, let's look at what being vulnerable is *not*. It's not sharing to create drama, get attention, or shock. The acronym 'TMI" for too much information has entered our everyday vocabulary—social media and the internet in particular have been like rocket fuel for this.

But in developing healthy relationships, expressing vulnerability in your communications is essential. It's how we build trust, intimacy, and connection. It's also liberating! You can be seen and understood for who you are.

Figure 2.2 Hands with written words that identify the person[7]

Imagine when your communication partner also has this experience. Now, you both have a safe space. You can have honest communication. You can genuinely give and receive empathy and understanding.

Nonetheless, being vulnerable in this way can be daunting. It can be misinterpreted as being soft, weak, or needy. Being vulnerable takes courage, strength, and the willingness to be uncomfortable to get the reward.

You may have strategies to block being vulnerable without fully realizing it. Here are some common ways people circumvent being vulnerable when communicating:

- *Hiding*: Keeping emotions concealed. Acting like one doesn't care or pretending to be positive when feeling something negative.
- *Avoiding*: Not bringing up or engaging in conversation when one feels triggered. Being 'too busy' to have the conversation.
- *Humor*: Making a joke. Being self-deprecating or making fun of the other person.
- *Pushing*: Being so critical of the other person that they just want to get away from the situation, and the person in it.

If you engage in any of these, whether in the extreme or with a lighter touch, and want to break this cycle, the next topic covers how to honor and express your emotions and needs.

Honoring And Expressing Genuine Emotions And Needs

Being 'genuine' is important here. As we've mentioned, masking or expressing the opposite of what you are feeling is a surefire way *not* to get far in having trust and understanding and short-circuits meaningful dialogue and deeper connections.

It's worth noting when you suppress emotions, they don't go away. Under these circumstances, as Richards and Gross have found, people have elevated blood pressure and higher levels of the stress hormone cortisol, which in turn negatively impacts memory during the event.[8] Imagine, "I don't remember it happening like that!" This doesn't bode well for mindful expressive communication.

Honoring and expressing emotions and needs in a genuine manner also doesn't mean falling for the trap of 'honesty is the best policy,' 'the truth hurts,' and so on. Those are excuses for not putting in the hard work of self-awareness, empathy, and trust.

Genuine emotions and needs are crucial in mindful communication because at their heart they promote vulnerability. When we are open and authentic, others see this and we can share each other's emotions. This is where empathy can thrive. When this happens, we can strengthen our relationships and have deeper connections.

And we know ourselves better. This process promotes our journey of self-discovery and personal growth. When we are strong and healthy in our identity, we have more to give others.

But how, exactly, can we be sure that we are expressing ourselves genuinely? Let's turn next to how you can go about capturing the potential of understanding and communicating your emotions and needs.

Identifying And Understanding Our Own Emotions

To identify and understand our emotions, it is helpful to first distinguish between basic and complex emotions.

Basic emotions are also called primary emotions. These are the feelings we first experience in life. They are almost automatic and come about immediately in reaction to an event. These are:

- Joy
- Surprise
- Fear
- Sadness
- Anger[9]

Next are complex or secondary emotions. These begin to be expressed once a child reaches about their third birthday. Then, throughout our development and into adulthood, they play a larger role.

Complex emotions do not replace basic emotions. Rather, they build on the basic emotions but differ in two key ways. They almost always have a relationship to the self— one of evaluation and often judgment and they are learned rather than instinctual. The pathway from simple to complex emotions is nicely explained by Olivia Guy-Evans of Simply Psychology:

- From Joy: Hope, Pride, Excitement, Delight
- From Surprise: Shock, Dismay, Confusion
- From Fear: Anxiety, Insecurity, Inferiority, Panic
- From Sadness: Shame, Guilt, Isolation, Depression
- From Anger: Annoyance, Resentment, Envy, Hate [9]

Each of the emotions is normal. What is key is how they are managed. For example, we all feel anger. Yet, if we were shut down when we expressed this emotion as a child and were told feeling angry is not acceptable, we may suppress this emotion in adulthood. On the other side of the spectrum, perhaps we witnessed our primary caregivers expressing anger inappropriately, whether directly through shouting or slamming doors, or passive-aggressively through thinly veiled criticisms. In both scenarios, we may never have learned how to appropriately express anger or other similar feelings with self-control and respect for others.

Human beings have an enormous capacity for emotions. You likely notice many of these emotions might be considered 'negative,' which is why it is important to delve into this topic as we discuss mindful expression. Many times, these emotions emerge when we feel we are not safe, when we feel we are being criticized or attacked, or when we are trapped in more violent communication patterns mired in conflict.

It can be understandable that we want to try to protect ourselves. This often materializes by fighting back with criticism, blame, and demands or shutting down and withdrawing. Both of these choices lead to resentment. They cause us to push others away. To keep relationships very superficial. The last thing we might be interested in is being vulnerable.

So, what techniques are available to you to recognize and label your emotions accurately?

- Think about basic and complex emotions and reflect on times when you felt each of these. It may be helpful to do this in the context of meditation or journaling.
- When you experience a strong emotion, take time to ask yourself why you are feeling it and what the deeper cause may be.
- Be sure to be kind to yourself and not try to judge whether you should be feeling the emotion.

Once you have a good handle on your own emotional understanding, the next big task is to communicate your needs effectively.

How To Effectively Communicate Needs

Remember that being able to communicate your needs

effectively is a core principle of nonviolent and mindful communication.

This process, too, begins with self-awareness. Take time to reflect on your own thoughts and feelings before expressing your needs. It's important to understand what you need and why it matters to you. By being clear about your needs, you can more effectively articulate them to yourself and to others.

To avoid misunderstandings, there are a few things to keep in mind. Be specific by clearly stating your needs and providing detailed information. You don't want to assume others know what you need—no one is a mind reader!

Establish boundaries by communicating them clearly while expressing your needs. Let others know what you can and cannot accept to ensure your needs are met respectfully. This is at the heart of being assertive—the balance between passive and aggressive.

When preparing to have communications, especially if they are highly charged, timing is king. Try to pick a time when you are calm, your communication partner is calm, and the setting is calm. This was a skill I worked hard to teach my two children when they wanted to bombard their dad with all the day's upsets when he had just arrived home from a long day at work!

It's fine as well when you convey that you need time to collect yourself. If the communication or interaction is positive for you having done so, your partner will learn to trust, and even encourage you rather than dread your return. What you are aiming for is to be able to maintain a calm and respectful demeanor.

During your interaction, you can call on the skill of active listening. This involves many of the techniques we have already discussed but let's go deeper here. I've also included this as one of the practice exercises coming up next.

Active listening builds trust, empathy, and meaningful connection. It is a powerful pathway to getting our needs met.

Give the other person your full attention and request the same. Pay attention to nonverbal communication, both in yourself and in the other person. Body language (e.g., eye contact, nodding, fidgeting, etc.) conveys a great deal, both positive and negative.

Use "I" statements by beginning your sentences with "I" to express your needs in a non-blaming and non-accusatory manner. Be mindful of making requests rather than demands. "I feel overwhelmed when I have too much to get down at once," rather than, "Can't you see I'm overwhelmed? You need to help me more!"

It's about the other person as well. Summarize what they are saying to ensure you understand their meaning. Ask questions if you need to clarify.

Share the emotions connected to your needs. Emotions can provide depth and context to your communication, helping others understand why meeting those needs is important to you.

Empathize with the other person's emotions as well. By understanding their perspective, you get insight into their feelings and points of view. Mindful expression is reciprocal.

Action Steps

<u>Exercises To Practice Mindful Communication</u>

This way of communicating may be new and unfamiliar to you. Therefore, it takes practice to gain competency. You can get primed and ready for the bigger event of difficult conversations by working out the kinks before the stakes are so high.

As we close this chapter, I want to offer you some exercises to help you become proficient in mindful expression to reduce conflict and encourage connection and collaboration.

Active Listening. This exercise can help improve listening skills, empathy, and communication practically and interactively.

1. Pair up with a friendly partner.

2. For the first round, determine who will be the speaker and who will be the listener.

3. For about two or three minutes, the speaker will talk

about a topic of their choosing. This could be something personal or a random topic.

4. The listener's goal is to practice active listening:

- Maintain eye contact and nod occasionally to show you're listening.
- Avoid interrupting the speaker.
- Use verbal cues like "I see," "I understand," or "Tell me more" to encourage the speaker.
- Reflect on what you've heard by paraphrasing or summarizing the speaker's main points.

5. Once the first round is finished, switch speaker and listener roles. Choose a new topic and repeat the exercise.

6. After both partners have had an opportunity to be the speaker and the listener, discuss the experience among yourselves. What did you learn about active listening? How did it feel to be listened to attentively?

Preparing For A Hard Conversation. This exercise can help you tackle difficult conversations, and perhaps trigger them by calling on being present, showing empathy, and having clarity. This can help you achieve more effective communication and successfully reach conflict resolution.

1. *Identify The Situation*: Determine what particular situation or issue you want to take on in the conversation. Jot down the main points that you want to cover.

2. *Connect With Your Feelings*: Allow yourself to consider what emotions are coming up for you. Describe your

feelings to yourself by using "I" statements. For example, "I feel guilty when..."

3. _Identify Your Needs_: Consider which of your needs are not being met. Write down the specific needs that are most important. For example, "I need to feel respected and heard..."

4. _Frame Your Request:_ Come up with a clear and specific request to make to the other person. These should be based on your feelings and your needs. Emphasize what you do want, and use positive language. Avoid focusing on what you don't want. For example, "I would feel more appreciated if you could..."

5. _Practice Empathy_: Put yourself in the other person's shoes. Try to understand their perspective. Write down possible reasons for their behavior or responses.

6. _Visualize The Conversation_: Quiet your mind and close your eyes. Now imagine engaging in the conversation. Visualize yourself staying calm, respectful, and empathizing with your communication partner throughout the interaction.

7. _Reflect:_ After the exercise, reflect on how you felt during the preparation. Did it help you feel more prepared and centered for the conversation? Where do you feel most confident? Where are you still unsure of yourself? Repeat the steps until you feel you have the best chance for success!

Chapter Summary

Whether it's talking with a co-worker like Brad, your parents and child like Joan, or any of the infinite scenarios where you are communicating with others, it can be challenging to do so in a positive way. By exploring the underpinnings of mindful expression, you can now better begin getting your needs met in respectful, peaceful, and fulfilling ways.

Key takeaways from this chapter are:

- When practicing mindfulness, to be successful you must understand its role in communication. You've learned this first necessitates deeply knowing yourself by being open to exploring what you are thinking and feeling and why.
- Vulnerability is the pathway to connection. It isn't a weakness to share your inner self—your feelings and your needs. Rather it takes courage and commitment.
- Mindfulness takes practice. By meditating, journaling, and connecting with nature, you have a roadmap to reach a positive state of mindfulness to use in communication interactions.
- Emotions are front and center when we experience and engage with the world. We set ourselves up for effective communication when we identify our emotions and feelings accurately and honestly.

- Self-awareness and self-control, being clear and detailed, setting boundaries, and using active listening with empathy are like the individual instruments in an orchestra. By practicing, you can enjoy a beautiful communication symphony!

As we have highlighted, self-awareness is vitally important for mindful communication. In chapter three, we will further delve into this aspect by introducing the concept of emotional intelligence. We will talk more about how to manage emotions effectively, particularly in the context of our personal biases.

3

RULE #2: USE THE POWER OF SELF-AWARENESS

HOW SELF-REFLECTION HELPS YOU MANAGE EMOTIONS AND BIASES WHEN COMMUNICATING

"Being aware of being aware of being. In other words, if I not only know that I AM but also know that I know it, then I belong to the human species." ~Vladimir Nabokov[1]

This quote from novelist Vladimir Nabokov accentuates that self-awareness is a uniquely human capacity. It is also a capacity that develops over the first few years of life and unfolds throughout our lifespan.[2]

The first step is to realize we are a separate and unique entity from our caregivers. During this time, we begin to understand we have free will. We realize that others do not share our unique thoughts and experiences.

We are also capable of the emotions we discussed in earlier chapters that have to do with the judgment of oneself, such as shame, guilt, and embarrassment. Additionally, this makes it possible to have an understanding of others. This opens the door to empathy.

Coming full circle to Nabokov's quote, we develop meta-cognition, which is when we can think about our thinking. Self-awareness is a powerful tool. To use it to its full potential, we must also strive to make optimal self-awareness a goal. This process can take many years, but with knowledge, experience, and effort, we can reach this potential more quickly. You are actively engaged in this process by reading this book!

Self-awareness isn't just about our general well-being and mental health; it has significant impacts on our day-to-day functioning.[3] Importantly, self-awareness is not static, it is dynamic.[2] It takes work and effort to attain and sustain. Mindfulness is a key aspect of this process. It allows us to handle demanding, and sometimes challenging, tasks—such as communication.

In this chapter, we will explore self-awareness for mindful expression and communication. We will delve more into effectively managing emotions. We will introduce emotional intelligence as a mechanism for mindful expression through self-awareness.

Our second rule to having good communication skills is to use the power of self-awareness.

Defining Self-Awareness, Emotional Intelligence, And Emotional Management

To set the stage, let's define the three core concepts that will form the basis of this chapter.

Beyond understanding that one is a separate entity from others, self-awareness is conscious knowledge of who you are as a person and a human being. It means you understand your own thoughts, emotions, motivations, desires, beliefs and values. You can think of it as your character. What do you stand for? What matters to you?

It also means that you are cognizant of how others see you and of how you see others. As human beings, we have a strong tendency to feel more affinity with those who are most similar to ourselves. This can serve as a safety net of sorts, but it also means we have a more difficult time accepting and relating to people whom we consider different. Emotional intelligence is a concept that directly taps into how we can better understand others.

While emotional intelligence might sound like a buzzword these days, research on emotional intelligence is actually more than a hundred years old.[4] In 1920, psychologist Edward Thorndike broached the idea of 'social intelligence'. This revolves around us understanding and managing our relationships with others.[5]

In the 90s, Peter Salovey and John Mayer coined the term 'emotional intelligence.' Emotional intelligence has many components. How we perceive our emotions, express them, use them, and manage them.[6]

What does it mean to be emotionally intelligent?

It means being able to understand and regulate or manage emotions in adaptive ways, resulting in more positive outcomes. Emotion management is difficult, especially in the case of unpleasant emotions.[7]

In the next two sections, we will take a closer look at what it means to effectively manage our emotions and how we can do so through self-reflection and emotional intelligence.

Managing Emotions Effectively

Managing emotions is termed "emotion regulation" by academics and researchers, so when you see that term, you will be aware of what it means. Emotion regulation goes back to responding in a way that is constructive and adaptive for the situation and what you want to accomplish. Most frequently, this is going to involve having control of how intense your feelings are and for how long those feelings go on.

Being emotionally intelligent does not mean suppressing your feelings. Rather it means that the emotions you experience can be expressed in ways that help you cope when you feel stressed, allow you to make clear-headed decisions, and support you in having strong and authentic connections with others.

Sociologist Christian Von Scheve offers interesting insight. He discusses the viewpoint of many researchers that why and how we manage emotions is couched in our personal cultural and social environment. What are the rules, values, and social practices expected of members of a particular society? These can have a substantial impact on how we are expected to behave emotionally.[7]

Yet, now we are much more citizens of the globe. Additionally, our social norms and expectations have loosened.[8] Extremely rigid rules have negative physical and mental impacts on how we express our emotions and behave. While these loosenings can be seen as positives, conversely, they have left many of us feeling unsettled and unsure, even if this may be subconscious. What is appropriate? What is acceptable? In other words, what are the boundaries?

Cultivating Self-Reflection And Emotional Intelligence

I believe this 'negative' feeling of being unsure and unsettled can represent a wonderful opportunity. It goes back to the discussion we had earlier about the emerging self. We have free will. This also means we have the power to be our best selves as we interact and communicate with others, no matter the situation.

We can achieve this through a deeper understanding of who we are as individuals by being self-aware. Through self-reflection, which starts with mindfulness, we are on our way to building emotionally intelligent skills. This includes managing our emotions, feeling empathy, and having positive social skills.

Let's turn next to how self-reflection and emotional intelligence intersect with mindful communication and authentic connections with others.

Emotion management begins with self-awareness. As we have discussed, self-awareness is being aware of your internal state and how you think others perceive you. The focus is on understanding yourself. It encompasses our values, beliefs, and emotions and where we have weaknesses and strengths.

Self-reflection is more closely related to mindfulness, which you have seen is about going inside yourself. When we engage in self-reflection, we review experiences from our past. This helps us gain insight so that we can learn from our past and improve going forward. Because every thought, emotion, experience, and interaction is always filtered through the self, managing your emotions by better understanding yourself both through self-awareness and self-reflection is key.

Self-reflection can help you tackle distorted thinking and break negative and destructive behavior patterns. In their article, "The Importance of Self-Reflection and Awareness for Human Development in Hard Times," Ardelt and Grunwald highlight that, as humans, we face more substantial challenges when situations are unpleasant, difficult, or even traumatic. This is when finding adaptive and constructive solutions counts the most.[9]

Let's now go more in-depth around self-awareness and what is known as cognitive reappraisal. You can do all the self-reflection in the world, but if that self-reflection means engaging in the same distorted thinking patterns, always having knee-jerk reactions to the same emotional triggers, and so on, it will mean continuing the identical behaviors that are detrimental.

We've talked previously about meditation, which means letting your thoughts come without judging. That is an important skill to learn, but it can't stop there if you want to move forward. The next step is to reframe your thinking. This is cognitive reappraisal, which refers to reframing how you interpret an event or situation so that you can change the impact it has on you emotionally. This strategy can result in more positive and less negative emotions and to having superior relationships with others.

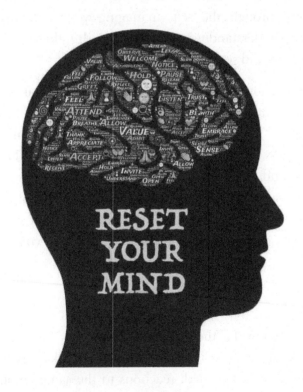

Figure 3.1 Cognitive reframing helps reset your mind to the positive[10]

It doesn't always mean you 'look for the silver lining' per se. Rather, it means you don't just automatically react as a result of the emotional response you immediately have to a challenging situation. It is true; you may be able to see the positive in the negative. But you might also see the reality, and it might not always be what you would like. The result, though, is a chance to learn, grow, and mature.

Let's take a look at how this can play out…

Janelle has been working hard on a side project for her friend Manuel, who is starting a new business. Janelle is hopeful she might be able to join the new company if she provides value and makes a good impression. However, Manuel sends her an email and, without explanation, drops it to Janelle that the project needs to be completed earlier than expected. Janelle feels overwhelmed and stressed, fearing that she won't be able to meet the new deadline. She feels a jolt of anger and then starts to experience increased anxiety. Doubtful thoughts about her abilities wash over her.

Janelle can feel herself falling into the same thought patterns she's had in the past in similar situations. "I can't do this." "What if I get fired because I have to spend more time right now on this side project?" "Why is Manuel such a jerk?" She is just about to type a snarky message back to her friend.

But Janelle has recently made friends with a co-worker who seems to handle high-pressure situations calmly and gracefully. Janelle has been getting tips from her, and doing some mindfulness and self-reflection exercises to improve her self-awareness. She's been learning to remind herself through self-reflection that she's been in this kind of pressure situation before, and she's come out on top.

Janelle takes a long shower and thinks about how this can showcase to Manuel her efficiency and adaptability. She decides she will practice self-compassion and that it's natural to feel overwhelmed, and even ticked off. She considers, too, that her friend probably didn't realize how his email would come across to Janelle and that he's under pressure with this project as well.

After this, Janelle feels slightly calmer and more focused. She gets out of the shower and does a few minutes of journaling, followed by a meditation with deep breathing. This really helps, but Janelle knows she also needs to get an action plan in place pronto. She opens her laptop and begins to outline the remaining tasks into manageable and prioritized steps. Janelle feels back in control. She is able to get a good night's sleep and the next morning gets a good bit completed before her day job starts.

Let's unpack how Janelle managed this, and how you can promote managing your emotions through self-reflection.

I encourage you to go back to activities we discussed in earlier chapters on mindfulness meditation and journaling. I want to provide a few others for you as well:

• *Tracking Emotions*: To help you identify patterns and triggers, keep a written or audio log of the emotions you are experiencing throughout the day. Do emotional check-ins with yourself throughout. Include the events or thoughts that triggered the emotions. It can be helpful to keep a list of emotions and their nuances so that you can refer to them as you do so. Go back through your log regularly to review your past emotions and the situations in which they occurred.

• *Emotion Regulation Strategies*: Develop strategies for how you have successfully managed your emotions. Was this meditation? Breathing exercises? Connecting with nature? Positive self-talk or affirmations? Turning your negative thoughts into positive ones? Think about situations where you used these, which were most effective, and where you still need work.

• *Set Goals*: As you identify where you would like to improve, be specific. Use your emotion tracking and emotional regulation strategies to help you pinpoint. Do you find that no matter your intentions, you lose your composure in the same way in the same situation? This is a great place to set a goal. Remember not to overwhelm yourself with too many goals at once. Otherwise, it will seem too daunting, and you might abandon the process. But also remember to celebrate your successes. As you see yourself making progress, and likely as others do as well, this will motivate you to keep going.

• *Share Your Feelings*: Much of the human experience is just that, human, because we are social beings. The truly important aspects of our lives happen in this context. Express your feelings verbally with others you trust. This can be cathartic, meaning it can lead to emotional healing. By talking things through and sharing how you feel, you can gain even further insight into yourself. You will also find a deeper connection with others.

Becoming self-aware through self-reflection is a mechanism that will enable you to better manage your emotions as you move through your daily experience. It will help you practice social skills that make communication and interaction more constructive and pleasant. It will allow you to feel empathy for others and form a closer and more authentic bond.

But what of interactions with others who are not such trusted allies, not in our 'inner circle'? Most of us frequently encounter people we do not know well. They may hold different values. They may have different customs. This can add another layer of challenge to mindful communication. Becoming emotionally intelligent can be much more daunting.

Recognizing And Managing Personal Biases And Judgments

Sociologist Monika Ardelt and mindfulness psychologist Sabine Grunwald discuss a number of theories of human development, including sociogenic models—a very compelling theory for mindful communication.[9]

Here, there is again a heavy influence on the deep connection we as humans have for social connection, but further, that we are driven to want to eliminate social injustices, such as disadvantages related to income, racism, sexism, and the like. According to this theory, when we can do this individually and collectively, we have reached our full potential.

However, we make judgments about others without really knowing them. We hold stereotypes. And... we often act on these biases, judgments, and stereotypes, resulting in failed communication. This poor communication cycle can spiral. At its best, this translates into a lack of genuine connection and, at its worst, into conflict and sometimes violence.

So, just what is personal bias?

This is when we hold a certain negative viewpoint about an individual or a group. This can result in an unfair attitude or behavior toward others or their ideas. How we come to hold these perspectives flows first from our upbringing as children. This is where our core values and beliefs are set. They become our reality.

They can also be quite automatic and occur without much thought when we encounter a trigger (a situation, event, etc.). The more kids are exposed to and use prejudice themselves, the more automatic it becomes, so it is entrenched by the teen years.[11]

Personal biases are taken with us into and throughout our adult lives. They are in play as we make decisions and as we interact with others. Yet, it is crucial to know that personal biases are learned. The good news follows—they can be unlearned!

The first step brings us back to metacognition. Remember: this is being aware of and understanding our own unique ways of thinking. Kleka and associates study what they refer to as the 'metacognitive self,' which is awareness of one's own biases. They write that, "…the need to acquire accurate knowledge about one's biases may result in metacognitive knowledge about the self."[12]

As we become adults, we have a drive to actively explore the self—our identity. Who are we? What do we stand for? How do we want to treat others? This can set us up for success in understanding and decreasing our biases through self-reflection because the metacognitive self helps us self-regulate emotions and behavior.

There are a plethora of types of biases. Keep in mind that a bias can be positive or negative. We will next look at some of these that particularly impact communication and relationships.

Stereotyping

This is the kind of bias we all have likely heard about. A stereotype is an oversimplified belief about a group of people, based on their characteristics. This could be gender, race, nationality, religion, and so forth. When we engage in stereotyping, we make assumptions. We think we understand an individual or group's habits, traits, or motivations. Stereotypes are founded on limited or even inaccurate information.

Stereotypes can put major roadblocks in the way of communication and positive relationships because we use them as justification for how we think about or behave toward others.[13] In other words, when we discriminate against an individual or group, we might rationalize that they 'deserve' such treatment. Our capacity for empathy —which, as we have discussed quite a lot, is crucial for strong relationships, is undermined.

Confirmation Bias

We discussed earlier as well that, as human beings, we tend to want to find or belong to our own 'tribe.' When we engage in confirmation bias, we seek validation for what we already believe. We seek out people who share our views. We read news that aligns with our beliefs. We go to talks where the speaker and topic are of personal interest.

Also related is in-group bias, where we prioritize those in our own group over others because we seek camaraderie. While this is understandable, the result of both these biases is that we are in a bubble, and as we mentioned before, the more we engage in the same thought and behavior patterns, the stronger our biases become. It becomes very challenging to hear another side and this immediately cuts off a chance for a meaningful relationship.

Availability And Anchoring Bias

A related set of biases are those of availability and anchoring, where we a) use what we know and don't bother to seek out new or different information, and/or b) just go with the first bit of information we come across, even if it is wrong or not relevant. When we follow these biases, we shut ourselves off from information that is vital for understanding, and therefore, connecting with others.

Negativity Bias And Halo Effect

When we engage in negativity bias, it is very much as it sounds. We pay more attention to negative experiences or information than to that which is positive. Conversely, the halo effect means that we view someone as exalted, and can do no wrong. We often make this assumption based on very limited traits or characteristics. Both can cause difficulty when forming relationships with others.

If we only see the negative, we may believe the other person does not care for us or does not hold us in high regard. Perhaps we see them as judgmental and critical. There is a lack of trust. None of these are a good breeding ground for closeness, and the result is loneliness.

Lemay and colleagues report strong evidence that loneliness related to negativity bias is associated with a host of undesirable outcomes. This ranges from lower psychological well-being, such as depression, to poorer performance in life activities like school and work, to physical health problems like poor sleep and illness.[14]

It is not necessarily a bad thing to see the best in someone. However, this halo effect can cloud your judgment about someone and spread to other aspects. For instance, if we think of someone as attractive physically, we may assume their character is also attractive when the two are unrelated. We also are more likely to make excuses when negative traits emerge.

On the flip side, it can be helpful in conflict because we may be more willing to give someone the benefit of the doubt, and forgive them. If a relationship is already strong, this can facilitate our willingness to stick it out and work on the relationship.

Let's take a closer look...

The neighborhood Tomas lives in has gotten more diverse over the years. As new people move in, he realizes he's believed for a long time that people from a certain cultural background aren't as hardworking. He bases this on how they maintain their lawns and vehicles, as Tomas is a stickler. However, as he's interacted with these folks more, he realizes that this stereotype is unfair. Tomas knows this in his head, but it feels like it's automatic. It's getting in the way of improving his relationships with his neighbors.

Tomas knows this particular group of neighbors gets together every weekend at a local park to play sports with their kids. Even though he feels uncomfortable, he decides to attend a game. Afterward, he chats with several people and meets their families. He waved to one or two but never introduced himself. One of the families invites Tomas back to their home for lunch.

He's hesitant at first, but finally says he'd like that very much.

At lunch, Tomas asks questions about their culture and their beliefs. He learns that a work-life balance is extremely important to them. They consider spending time with their children, in particular, to be one of the most sacred responsibilities they have. Tomas has a flash of insight that his negative view of not being hardworking is related to his neighbors not spending all their free time like he does mowing their lawns and washing their cars. Now, he gets it and finds himself admiring them for this commitment to building strong relationships within their families.

Figure 3.2 A father and son hugging.[15]

When we are willing to be more self-aware about our personal biases and lapses in judgments, explore them, and face them head-on, we have a much greater chance to achieve that positive, strong social connection we all need. Through self-reflection, we build the emotional intelligence skills that will allow us to navigate our communications and ensure they are more constructive and adaptive.

Action Steps

A key to overcoming bias and growing closer to self-awareness and emotional intelligence is open-mindedness:

- To suspend judgment.
- To see the world through another's perspective.
- To develop empathy.

Here are some techniques you can use to help you in this process.

Mindfulness: Practice the mindfulness techniques we've shared, reflecting without judgment on experiences where you encounter biases within yourself. Write down the biases you notice you're susceptible to and your plan to overcome them.

Education. Look for reputable and balanced books, documentaries, or workshops on bias (those related to inclusion and diversity can be helpful). Do a media awareness check by asking yourself if they engage in stereotyping, negative bias, or the halo effect.

Broaden Interactions. Find opportunities to interact with the people whom you hold stereotypes and other biases about. Attend cultural festivals. Volunteer in neighborhood community centers different from your own. Invite someone from a different background to get a cup of coffee and chat.

Chapter Summary

As we come to the end of this chapter and reflect on "being aware of being aware of being," we can put the pieces together of self-awareness, emotion management, emotional intelligence, and personal bias. We can now see how they interact to help us as we navigate social interactions to create strong, meaningful relationships. In essence, to be a part of the human species in all the best ways.

Key takeaways for you are:

- Self-awareness allows us to dig deep within ourselves to understand not just our thoughts and emotions, but also our values and beliefs. Our values and beliefs can be highly charged with emotion because they make up who we are —our identity. As we learn to regulate these emotions, they do not lose their meaning, but the intensity and the duration are now more under our control. We can harness them in ways that are healthier and more constructive.

- These fit in as puzzle pieces in our emotional intelligence. As we better understand ourselves, we can better understand others through empathy. Our social skills improve. We can now interact with others in a manner that is more authentic and genuine.

- But we must be vigilant of our biases. These can come in, often automatically, to derail these efforts. By knowing more about the types of biases that exist in interpersonal relationships, why we might hold them, and how they manifest, we can overcome them using active and thoughtful techniques.

Doing so takes work. It can be slow and hardgoing. But the result is that we fulfill our drive as humans to not only have more positive personal relationships but also carry forward the cause of ensuring all of us are treated fairly and humanely.

What we say, what we hear others say, how we react, and how we interpret how others respond is where communication becomes real and concrete. In the next chapter, we will revisit active listening as a technique. We will take a deeper dive and examine how to firmly master this approach.

4

RULE #3: DON'T JUST HEAR—BUT LISTEN!

HOW GOING FROM HEARING TO UNDERSTANDING TRANSFORMS THE CONVERSATIONS YOU MAKE

C al's wife passed away three years ago. Now, he is a single father to his daughter Emily, who just turned 13. This was a traumatic event that brought Cal and Emily very close. Yet there's been a growing distance between them recently. He knows becoming a teen comes with challenges. Emily seems moodier, and she's pushing for more independence. Adding fuel to the fire, she's having a hard time accepting that Cal has recently started dating. Cal is struggling to communicate with her effectively.

One evening, Cal decides to start yet another conversation with Emily about her day at school, but she again responds with one-word answers and seems disinterested. Cal blurts out, "You never want to talk to me! You're really turning into a brat!" Emily's eyes get big, and tears begin to form. She runs out of the room, and he hears her bedroom door slam. Cal feels increasingly frustrated and unsure of how to connect with his daughter. He worries that he is losing touch with her, and their once-strong bond is slipping away.

Figure 4.1 A father looking pensive about how to talk to his child.[1]

The third rule to having great conversations is to listen, and not just hear.

I chose this scenario because the term 'active listening' was coined by Thomas Gordon in the 70s and is a core basis for his approach and extremely popular books on Parent Effectiveness Training.[2] When I was an undergraduate getting my degree in child development, this was a required reading. In my master's in education and several years later in my PhD in psychology, it was still going strong.

Today, active listening for parents has evolved into 'mindful parenting.' This is where the relationship quality is improved through parents being more self-aware of their thoughts, emotions, and behaviors and by interacting and communicating with their child in an intentional way, in the present moment, patient, and nonjudgmental.[3]

With regard to active listening specifically, not only has it become entrenched in dealing with parent-child relationships, but has spread far and wide into other situations. It is a staple of communication training in personal or professional relationships. We can find the practice of active listening employed in marriage counseling, teaching, healthcare, management training, and hostage negotiation, to name a few. Through active listening, we are able to understand one another more deeply.

Circling back to mindfulness, researchers are now exploring how this interacts with active listening in a broader sense, particularly with regard to empathy and perceptions of emotional support. Susanne Jones and her associates research supportive communication. They studied how the various aspects of mindfulness play a significant part in supportive communication. The authors note that providing emotional support to others comes at a cost. This may be experiencing stress, feeling responsible, or having negative emotions.[4] It can be draining!

However, we can better deal with the emotions of others if we are objectively mindful and recognize and accept our emotions. Additionally, as we do so, we are better able to put ourselves in someone else's shoes and feel empathy.

Defining Active Listening

Figure 4.2 A couple having a lively conversation.[5]

We introduced active listening in an earlier chapter, but let's refresh our memories. Active listening is a communication technique and approach. When we engage in active listening, we concentrate fully on what the other person is saying. We have the goal to effectively understand, remember, and respond to their words and to their nonverbal cues alike.

In communication interaction where active listening is in play, both parties feel genuinely heard. They believe they are being taken seriously. This leads to feeling respected and valued. Such feelings make trust possible.

Both parties feel clearer about their feelings, thoughts, and needs. As questions are posed, new information is learned, and the air is 'cleared.' Now, insights and cognitive reappraisal can happen. Once there is more clarity, both parties can likely articulate their needs, and the relationship can advance in a positive manner.

There are many parallels between active listening and emotional intelligence as well. In both active listening and emotional intelligence skills, we must recognize a wide variety of emotions. These emotions must be regulated, and empathy is a core element. This allows us to build stronger relationships with others, particularly in our daily lives. You can likely see how mindfulness would be an asset!

Active listening and emotional intelligence both shore up our general social skills. When we can build rapport and show sensitivity and awareness, we are able to thrive in social situations. Listeners who are seen as effective leave more positive impressions, come across as trustworthy, and are seen as socially attractive—which means people want to spend time with them.[6]

The Components And Stages Of Active Listening

The key elements of active listening are paying attention, showing interest, clarifying, reflecting feelings, and summarizing. Let's first take a moment to understand that we don't just fall into the active listening technique.

Active, or effective listening as it is sometimes called, typically follows a progression and a cycle. Judi Brownell is a professor and researcher in listening behavior and leadership, she has developed the **HURIER** model, which is useful in helping us understand how this looks.[7] HURIER has the following components and stages:

Hearing. A person first decides what to focus on and what to ignore. If someone is on their phone while you are trying to have a serious conversation and they are distracted, you can relate to the importance of this!

Understanding: The listener now must have the language and comprehension skills to understand the actual words being spoken. If your communication partner speaks another language, for example, this can impact understanding. We might also have experience communicating with young children who do not yet have the cognitive skills to articulate clearly or understand what is said to them fully.

Remembering: Next, the listener must be able to remember the information being shared to respond appropriately. This takes cognitive energy. We have to be actively engaged in working with the information in our minds to keep it there and to recall it later.

Interpreting: Now, we have to take in both verbal and nonverbal cues and give them meaning. We have to attend to the actual words as information and aspects like someone's tone of voice, facial expressions, and the situational context. If someone is saying, "I'm fine!" but they are being curt or have a pained facial expression, chances are they are not fine.

Evaluating: Related to this is evaluation, where we have to determine the accuracy and validity of the information received. We weigh up all the evidence so to speak. It is crucial that the message is felt to be understood before we judge its value. We may need to get or give more clarification.

Responding: Finally, we reach the outcome of active listening—we can give an appropriate response. As the response is being given, the communicator may be adjusting. Our partner's facial expressions, tone of voice when responding, and so on tell us how well we are hitting the mark of effective listening. We want to be open to realizing we might not get it right out of the gate! [7]

Situations Where Active Listening Matters

Active listening can be used in any communication situation, but is especially powerful in difficult or sensitive conversations, including:

Personal Relationships. When communicating in intimate relationships with our romantic partner, family, children, or best friends, these conversations can be particularly charged with emotions. Not only do we feel our most vulnerable, but the need to have trust is at its highest. Poor communication shuts this down, as we saw in the scenario with Cal and Emily.

Performance Feedback. If you have ever received or given feedback in a professional relationship, you can likely recall the anxiety you might have felt if there is going to be an element of criticism or negative feedback. Active listening can help ensure the goal of improved performance is achieved.

Diversity and Inclusion. As discussed at length previously, conversations in this area come with many land mines. By using active listening, we are able to understand and appropriately respond to different perspectives and experiences without bias and instead with empathy.

Controversial Topics. Respect and being open to other points of view can be challenging when discussing topics around politics, policy, or religion, for example. Active listening techniques allow you to have a meaningful conversation rather than digging your heels in on your position.

Conflict Resolution. In situations where there is conflict, there is typically anger. While anger is a natural human emotion, it makes communicating effectively next to impossible. This is where active listening can help with emotion regulation so you can express your feelings more constructively.

Barriers To Effective Active Listening

We have mentioned barriers such as distractions, language, cognitive capacity, biases, and unregulated emotions, but I would like to spend some time looking at two unexpected areas that are stumbling blocks even for folks trained in active listening. Following this, we will address barriers that are more commonly recognized.

Joseph Topornycky and Shaya Golparian are educational consultants who conduct needs assessments, develop workshops, and carry out program evaluations. They began to see that active listening, which they also refer to as empathetic listening, was sometimes misused. This undermined the true intent of active listening. The two key stumbling blocks they found are 'parroting' and 'projecting.'[8]

<u>Parroting</u>

As we highlight the importance of repeating what someone says, we need to be aware that just doing this is not listening. It is termed parroting—similar to how a parrot repeats verbatim or imitates a behavior.

Listening is more subtle...and more complex. It is what we do as humans when we take in information (verbal and nonverbal) and combine that with the other components we discussed, such as understanding and interpreting.

When you parrot what someone is saying, they will catch on. They may tell you they think you're 'just going through the motions.' You come across as less authentic and genuine. They aren't going to believe you are interested in connecting with them.

When you repeat, your intent is to help your communication partner know they were understood. You will likely want to expand to reach this goal. Rather than, "What I hear you say is Samantha really made you mad," you might try, "It sounds like you got really mad when Samantha did that. Why do you think she acted that way toward you?" Now you have shown that you heard your friend and are interested in going further than the surface level.

Projecting

The second stumbling block Topornycky and Golparian found was projecting. When we try to make sense of something, we have a superpower as humans. We have the capacity to connect it to previous learning. This is one of the ways we, as humans, are so skilled at advancing our knowledge.

However, there is a downside. As we saw in the previous chapter, this can result in bias—and in a way, this happens when we project. It's almost the opposite of empathy. Instead of objectively imagining what the other person is feeling, we tend to view their situation through our experiences.

It could be that we are very much aligned, but just as frequently, it could be we are not. Putting our personal beliefs, values, or experience into the mix, can backfire if we aren't careful. Think of the parent who says, "When I was your age....," the friend who says, "I would never put up with that! You don't think you should either, do you?" or the boss who says, "I know it's tough to be starting out in a new company, but I managed it, and I know you can get up to speed with how we do things around here."

Instead, your role in active listening is to be a guide on a journey to help the other person clarify what they are feeling and to come to a resolution. This resolution may not be anything more than cognitive reappraisal, or it might involve taking some drastic action. The most important outcome is one in which their needs are met in a way that works for them.

Now, let's look at some of the more obvious barriers to active listening.

<u>Interrupting</u>

I can relate to this one as I have a daughter who is quite sensitive to this. She likes to get it all out before I respond. Sometimes I find myself wanting to paraphrase or just to respond in some way so she knows I am listening. Yet to her, the most powerful way this is conveyed is silence so she can express herself fully. If you are tempted to interrupt, hold back. It can be amazing what this space and being patient will allow the other person to share.

<u>Being Emotionally Upset</u>

When we are angry, anxious, upset, or sad, we will have difficulty listening and speaking. While it may be too much to expect to wait until these feelings are completely gone, if they are interfering to the point where we cannot get through a conversation, it is fine to take breaks. Not everything has to be resolved in a single conversation— likely for topics that matter, this isn't even realistic.

<u>Confusing Active Listening With Seeking Advice</u>

We just discussed that active listening is about someone coming to their own conclusions. Yet, there are times when we have communication needs that are about seeking advice—plain and simple. Have you ever had a salesperson be too empathetic? Lots of: "I understand." "That must be hard." "It sounds like you are really unhappy?" when all you want is to gather information or get some advice on the best car to purchase for your situation! There may be times when someone just wants advice.

Your Active Listening Needs

When trying to get your needs met, keep in mind the person on the other side of the conversation may have never heard of active listening, much less how to practice it. While it can seem like a big lift, you may find that you have to help them help you. You can talk with them about what you've learned and how important it is to work on your communication skills to have a strong and healthy relationship with them.

Figure 4.3 A couple in serious conversation.[9]

In addition to practicing the various elements of active listening, let's revisit how mindfulness can help you as well. The Five-Facet Mindfulness Questionnaire is a frequently used scale to measure mindfulness developed by Baer and colleagues.[10] It captures the following five key components, which you can use to keep yourself grounded as you engage in active listening.

- *Observing*: attending to internal and external stimuli (thoughts, memories, feelings, physical sensations).
- *Aware acting*: attending to our actions at the moment, in real-time, rather than responding automatically.
- *Describing*: labeling and expressing our experiences.
- *Nonjudging*: refraining from evaluating our thoughts and emotions.
- *Nonreacting*: not getting caught up in our emotions.

Revisiting Our Scenario

Now that we have unpacked active listening, let's revisit Cal and Emily.

Even though he feels frustration, Cal focuses on taking a step back to reflect on the situation. He realizes he needs to find a different way to approach Emily and better ways to communicate with her. The next day, Cal sits down with Emily and first apologizes. Then, he gently shares his concerns. Cal tells Emily she is the most important person in his life. He shares how much he values their relationship and wants to understand her better.

To his surprise, Emily opens up about her feelings of confusion and insecurity as she navigates adolescence. She explains she often feels overwhelmed and doesn't know how to talk to her dad about her struggles. She shares her feelings that if he has a girlfriend, not only will he forget her mom, he also won't have any time for her. Cal listens attentively, validating Emily's feelings and offering his support.

Over time, Cal and Emily work on their communication skills together. They establish regular check-ins to discuss the big and small things in their lives. Cal learns to listen actively, without judgment, and asks Emily questions to understand her feelings and thoughts. As a result, Emily feels more comfortable expressing herself openly.

Through patience, understanding, and a willingness to adapt, Cal and Emily strengthen their relationship and overcome the communication challenges they once faced. Cal learns that effective communication requires empathy, active listening, and a genuine desire to connect with his daughter, and Emily learns that her dad is always there for her, no matter what.

Active Listening In Digital Communications

For our last major topic in this chapter, let's turn to how active listening is relevant when communicating in our ever-increasing digital world. Many of us communicate primarily through channels such as emails, text messages, and instant messaging platforms. We have seen the rise of emojis, and now, AI (artificial intelligence) programs are popping up that can help us write emails in a variety of ways, like being more friendly or more motivational. It's clear we all are looking for ways to connect in our digital relationships.

There are scores of studies on the potential for miscommunication in personal and professional relationships when using digital communication.[10] Studies have found digital communication is seen as more impersonal, the formation of trust is delayed, and people are less accurate in interpreting the emotions of others. On the flip side, there are some positives, according to research, such as higher social attractiveness and being more open to sharing one's emotions and information about oneself, as it can feel anonymous and therefore, less threatening.

Christine Bauer and colleagues study the interaction of humans with intelligent systems. They were interested in the limitations and the benefits of digital communication. They studied active listening in instant messaging and email. Regarding the overall limitations, active listening, which can already feel like a commitment, may be seen as more burdensome because even extra effort has to go into it in a digital setting.[10]

Not surprisingly, the loss of nonverbal cues was present. Interestingly, it was more of a negative in email than text messages because the former had a delayed response while the latter was more immediate and so people felt the social presence of the other person more fully. In instant messaging, the messages can overlap, which is akin to interrupting. We've also likely been a little impatient and annoyed waiting while it looks like someone is typing and nothing comes!

So, can you apply active listening in a digital environment?

Yes. Face-to-face communication is still best if possible for high-stakes situations, but there are several strategies you can use when communicating digitally to promote active listening.

Take Your Time

If there is a need for active listening, it deserves time and effort. Taking it seriously, engaging fully and mindfully, and avoiding cliches like "I understand" are key. Imagine how you would behave in person and try to mirror that in your digital communication.

Ask For More Context

Having a running log of the conversation can be helpful, but if you need more information, let the other person know this in a respectful way. Rather than, "I have no idea what your issue is," try, "I want to make sure I understand your situation. Can you give me a bit more information?"

Use Graphics

You can lighten a mood, show solidarity, and convey that you are there for someone who is struggling by using emojis, memes, and so on. Be careful, though, as there is room for miscommunication here as well. People of different generations and cultures may interpret these graphics very differently from those in your peer group.[11]

Action Steps

<u>Exercises To Hone Active Listening Skills</u>

Here are some specific exercises to help you practice active listening.

• *Mindful Listening*. Practice listening without interrupting verbally. Increase your toolbox of nonverbal cues, such as nodding, mirroring the other person's body language, or offering a gentle touch if appropriate.

• *Reflective Listening*. Practice repeating what you heard but in your own words. Concentrate on capturing the essence of what your conversation partner is saying, including their feelings and intentions. Summarize at the end to highlight the main points.

• *Get Feedback*. It might feel intimidating, but share with others that you are working on your communication skills. Ask for constructive feedback to help you pinpoint areas where you can improve.

• *Previous Activities*. Establish the habit of the various mindfulness activities we have shared so far, including meditation, connecting with nature, self-care, and journaling. Find partners to do the Active Listening Activity and the Preparing for Hard Conversations shared in Chapter 2.

Chapter Summary

Built on empathy and emotional support, active listening is a powerful communication technique and has made its way into a wide array of settings and situations. While active listening takes time and effort, and there are challenges and limitations, the benefits are enormous for helping build strong, meaningful relationships.

Here are the key takeaways for you:

- In active listening, the communication partners fully concentrate, understand, respond, and remember what is being said in conversation. They attend to and give verbal and nonverbal feedback to show understanding and encourage further communication.
- The HURIER model can help you through the active listening process. HURIER stands for hearing, understanding, remembering, interpreting, evaluating, and responding.
- Active listening is particularly useful in challenging situations such as personal relationships, performance reviews, controversial topics, conflict, and virtual communication. It helps us feel respected and valued and we are more likely to be our more authentic selves — which promotes trust.
- You can improve your active listening skills by using a number of strategies, such as

mindfulness, reflective listening, role-play, and seeking feedback.

In the next chapter, we will explore how embracing diversity and practicing cultural sensitivity can promote nonviolent communication.

5

RULE #4: ALL ABOUT EMPATHY AND CULTURAL INTELLIGENCE

HOW BEING PROFICIENT IN THESE CONCEPTS CAN HELP YOU COMMUNICATE BETTER

"Culture reinforces the economic, social, and communal fabrics that regulate social cohesion. Communication helps to maintain social order." ~ Stella Aririguzoh[1]

This quote from Stella Aririguzoh, a mass communications researcher and lecturer, is a gripping reminder of the stakes at hand when addressing cross-cultural communication.[1]

In this chapter, we will explore the relationship between diversity and cultural sensitivity and the role these play in supporting nonviolent communication.

As a consultant, I have had the privilege of working with clients across the globe. I have also seen many opportunities where a project is only available to a consultant from a certain country or region. To me, this highlights that while the internet, in particular, has allowed us all to be citizens of the globe, this is in name only. Truly connecting with others from different cultures is much more complex.

As human beings, we all have a strong drive to communicate. We want to be heard. To be understood. And we want this to happen in a respectful way. As we discussed, notably in chapter one, this is at the heart of nonviolent communication.

That said, we all come to a communication interaction with who we are, and culture is a core element. Culture is learned and encompasses our values, beliefs, and customs. It manifests through our ethnic affiliation, religion, art, child-rearing, and more.

Effective communication is not about stripping this away. Not only is it impossible, it is not desirable. Rather, we want to embrace our diversity and that of others and effectively and mindfully communicate within the context of cultural sensitivity. Similarly to emotional intelligence, we can think of this as 'cultural intelligence' as introduced by business researchers Christopher Earley and Elaine Mosakowski.[2]

Rule number four states, "Practice empathy and cultural intelligence to be an effective communicator."

Workplace and education settings are two areas where we are likely to interact with others from differing cultures. Let's take a closer look.

<u>Workplace</u>

To be competitive, companies must often be global. This will result in not just selling into these markets but also having employees from them. In a large review of 60 studies, Rebecca Merkin and colleagues did a deep dive and found that problems with communication constitute one of the greatest challenges in business. This ranged from mistranslations to misunderstandings to suspiciousness. The result is often conflict.[3]

While many companies will provide training in language or cultural knowledge, these are only part of a successful equation. Mindful communication is a vitally important component. Without this, we may have 'book knowledge,' but we will not be able to apply this successfully in ways that promote positive outcomes. In other words, we will fall short of cultural intelligence.

Education

Educational settings also see individuals from many diverse cultures as part of their student bodies. There are many obstacles and challenges that emerge when cultural intelligence is missing from the equation, where we do not have empathy and understanding, and a broader worldview. This often happens with the rationale that such topics are 'divisive concepts.'[4]

But in reality, the whole point is that such curricula and programs are intended to make these topics *less* divisive. The Center for Mindfulness, Compassion, and Resilience at Arizona State University in the USA has put forth the 'Equitable Mindfulness' framework.

This emerged from a need to recognize the multicultural nature of education with the goal of helping faculty navigate difficult conversations around inclusion and equity policies and practices. The framework was developed to "promote personal and societal introspection while bridging gaps between communities and breaking down barriers against inclusive practices."[5]

In particular, the members of the Center are increasingly concerned as they observe emotions such as anger and hurt. Seeing individuals suffering from feelings of isolation. Watching the growing political polarization. And finally, the need for human connection and healing that is being undermined when diversity, inclusion, and equity are trampled.

Yet, we as individuals have the choice to be culturally sensitive. That can be exceptionally powerful!

Cultural Intelligence

Let's now turn our attention more fully to mindful communication as a tool for cultural sensitivity. There are several major elements of cultural intelligence.[6] They have much in common with mindful communication.

Metacognitive

Here, as we interact with others from different cultures, we work to be more aware of their preferences and intentions. We observe and revise our knowledge along the way.

Motivational

We are interested in learning about and participating in cultural diversity. The more we do so, the more confident we become as we communicate sensitively with others from varying cultures.

Behavioral

We put our cultural intelligence into action. We are able to communicate verbally and nonverbally (such as gestures and physical space) in appropriate ways. We are aware enough to change these depending on the various situations in which we find ourselves.

When we practice mindful communication in the context of cultural intelligence, there are many benefits. The overarching one is that not only will we have better day-to-day personal interactions, but we are better poised to be outstanding global citizens in a connected world.

As we are exposed to more diverse viewpoints, our knowledge base increases. We can learn different ways of thinking, feeling, behaving—of being. It really cannot be understated that how humans have advanced is also due to our ability to work together. Our capacity to take on and solve complex problems; to discover and invent, to experience better health, economics, and diplomacy with other nations, not to mention aspects such as art and music that enrich our lives.

Figure 5 People considering the diverse world we live in.[7]

Communication Styles, Values, and Norms

Awareness of some of the differences among cultures can help us as we communicate. Individualistic cultures, often Western, value personal goals while those that are more collective, such as Eastern, African, and South American, value the goals of the group. Some cultures have differing power dynamics, being more masculine or feminine-driven or seeing more of a hierarchy among boss and employee, teacher and student, and so on. Some cultures value protocol around structure and rules more than others.

Let's look at some concrete examples of how this could play out...

<u>Touching</u>

In some cultures, it is acceptable to have physical contact, sometimes rather intimate. For example, it is the national custom in France to hug and kiss on both cheeks. However, this can make other cultures very uncomfortable, particularly with the opposite sex. A good rule of thumb is not to initiate any physical contact. If the other party does so and you are comfortable, you can engage.

<u>Dress</u>

Casual Friday is the norm in many business settings and can go far in some companies. However, some cultures would find shorts and a T-shirt in the office to be inappropriate, especially if they are revealing. In some cultures, people dress more formally, even just going out to run errands, while in others, the norm is to be more casual, with workout clothes perfectly acceptable for instance. Doing your research can help you find the middle ground, but if you are still not sure, you would want to dress up, not down, especially with superiors.

<u>Time</u>

In Germany for instance, punctuality is highly prized while in other parts of the world it is much looser. For example, Saudi Arabia, India, Nigeria, and Kenya value flexible time.[8] Depending on whom you are communicating with, you would either want to be on time or even early, or be more flexible and relaxed.

<u>Language</u>

There are a seemingly infinite number of nuances in language, as well as how formal or informal we can be when speaking. It's best to be cautious about using jargon or slang and avoid profanity.

The Bridge Of Empathy

If communication is our common territory, empathy is the bridge that gets us there. Empathy can open us up to understanding cultural norms. It helps us deal with challenges and resolve conflict. Empathy builds trust and collaboration in our cross-cultural communications. Let's see how this might play out…

Josephine works for a multinational corporation headquartered in New York and is going to Japan to meet with potential partners to launch a new product in this market. She's had some language training, learned about the culture as much as she can, and has been focusing on going through this experience with empathy at the top of mind as she navigates what might be a delicate negotiation.

As she expected, Josephine noticed her Japanese colleagues are fairly reserved. They tend to listen rather than talk a great deal. This is different from her style, which is to speak at length and quickly. She makes it a point to speak slowly and pause so her counterparts can process the information she shares.

When there is a pricing disagreement, though, Josephine reflexively voices her displeasure and immediately realizes that she has offended her potential partners. She quickly apologizes, actively listens, and finds that she is empathetic to their needs.

While it was still a challenging day, Josephine is excited to be invited to a traditional tea ceremony. She knows this is one of the ways the Japanese business culture works. Josephine puts her worries aside and leans into showing respect for the local customs.

By being open to understanding and respecting Japanese culture, her hosts let her know they appreciate her efforts. The team is able to work through the details and come to a compromise. Now, they are working toward a successful product launch in this new market in Japan.

Overcoming Stereotypes And Biases In Cross-Cultural Communication

Josephine navigated her situation with empathy, but as discussed in the chapter on biases, these can derail those efforts for many of us.

Stereotypes about people from other cultures are one of the most common obstacles for us because we may think we are less like people from other cultures. This opens the door for prejudice and discrimination. As we discussed previously, we may find we can rationalize our behavior as we disregard their feelings and needs, not to mention what they are able to contribute. The result can be hostility and even violence.

We can bridge these divides through empathetic dialogue. When we employ mindfulness and active listening, we can break down these barriers. We can foster respect and harmony. We can have meaningful connections so that everyone's needs are met.

Practicing Empathetic Listening

Let's look at how nonviolent communication can build understanding and trust in communication, rather than breed hostility and conflict.

Active Listening

The previous chapter can help you practice active listening. Yet, when communicating with someone from another culture, you will also want to consider the communication styles, values, and norms we discussed and apply them while listening actively.

Open-Mindedness

Putting your biases and preconceptions aside is vital. Creating inclusive and respectful dialogue means being receptive to new ideas and ways of viewing the world. Reading, watching videos, and attending workshops and lectures can give you a foundation. Asking your communication partner questions, visiting their homes and communities, and reciprocating can expand your skills.

Perspective-Taking

Understandably, we view the world through our experiences, values, and beliefs. But for empathetic dialogue, even though it takes effort, we will want to try to imagine how someone from another culture sees the world.

A further note is that we may tend to hear 'culture' and think of someone living in a different part of the world. However, even within the same country, of course there will be many cultures. This is especially true in countries with larger populations.

One place we see this play out is immigration. Lauren McLaren is a professor of politics and notes, "Since the end of World War II, immigration has become one of the most divisive issues on the political agendas of Western democracies".[8] She discusses that many of us find it extremely challenging to think about how our nation looks and functions, when people come in, whom we believe do not share our values.

Her research confirms that how our political leaders handle this–welcoming or labeling as a threat–impacts how its citizens respond.[8] If you find yourself living in a nation where the latter is true, again, if you genuinely want to connect in a positive and healthy manner, you may have to take up that charge individually.

Cross-Cultural Global Communication And Digital Platforms

We spoke in the last chapter about using active listening in a digital setting. Perhaps nowhere has the capacity for global communication become more possible than through our advances in digital communication. We now have a torrent of goods, services, data, jobs, healthcare, entertainment, social connections, and more coming through these channels. From individuals to mammoth corporations, cross-cultural digital communication is not only here to stay. It's growing by leaps and bounds.

So, how can we ensure mindful communication in such a setting?

First, we don't lose sight of the goal of cross-cultural communication, which is to improve our interactions. Second, we are aware of the potential for miscommunication. Third, we employ all we have learned in this chapter about cultural intelligence and empathetic listening. All of these foster rapport and a sense of trust.

But we can add a fourth—the amazing technology tools we have at our disposal! These can put us on a level playing field with our communication partners no matter who or where they are.

Business school researchers Denys Lifintsev and Wanja Wellbrock studied the impact of digitalization on cross-cultural communication. They found email, social networks, instant messenger, and the like make cross-cultural communication easier. It was faster and more accessible.

You may be surprised to find this research revealed that the impersonal nature of digital communication was an advantage. Why? Communication was not as affected by the nuances and particulars that come into play when we communicate face-to-face.

Further, the language barrier was actually less. First, people have more time and less pressure to read, process, and respond. Second, there is an opportunity to use translation programs. Third, as we discussed in the previous chapter, more tools are available like auto-correct and digital writing assistants. You can also incorporate visual aids. Pictures and diagrams can convey meaning to your communication partner.[9] As you find yourself in cross-cultural communication, I encourage you to take advantage of these tools.

Action Steps

Working to cultivate empathy can make all the difference in having meaningful cross-cultural communication, whether in business, school, or personal relationships. To develop the bridge of empathy, in addition to active listening, here are some activities for you.

• *Self-Reflection Questions*: Ask yourself questions, like: How are my perceptions of others influenced by my own cultural values? When I am interacting, how can I show respect for cultural differences? How can I adapt my communication style to be more inclusive of different cultural norms, values, beliefs, etc.?

• *Learn*: Educate yourself about different cultures. Find books and articles to read. Watch documentaries. Go to talks. Attend events and festivals. Learn basic phrases in different languages.

• *Cultural Sensitivity Training*: Sign up for workshops or classes that focus on cultural sensitivity. Look for those that are practice-based where you can do role-plays, journaling, field trips, and practice speaking with others from different cultural backgrounds.

Chapter Summary

In this chapter, we have tackled a topic that could be considered sensitive, and hopefully done so in a sensitive manner!

You will be better positioned to be effective at nonviolent and mindful communication by embracing diversity and cultural sensitivity. By applying your newfound knowledge about the roadblocks and the strategies to overcome them, you can navigate your way more successfully in cross-cultural communication and create meaningful connections.

Here are key takeaways for you:

- We live in a globally connected world and will face differences. Embracing rather than avoiding supports authentic connections.

- Cultural intelligence helps avoid stereotypes and biases through empathy and open-mindedness, leading to respect and trust.
- Techniques to address barriers, such as active listening, self-reflection, and formal learning opportunities, support communication face-to-face and digitally.
- Not everyone may share your desire for genuine connections with different cultures. Just remember, you don't need anyone's permission to practice empathy and cultural sensitivity.

In the following chapter, we will tackle conflict. We will talk about why situations of conflict arise and how to resolve these in a way that is both constructive and peaceful using mindful communication.

6

RULE #5: DON'T BE AFRAID TO FACE CONFLICTS!

HOW TO KILL CONFLICTS WITH KINDNESS... AND GOOD COMMUNICATION SKILLS!

When I was a girl, my sister, who was several years older and newly married, would buy a new romance novel at the supermarket checkout every week without fail. I was curious as to the appeal, as well as intrigued as to how new books could be available so fast. When I got older, I read several of the books in her now extensive library.

It didn't take long to discover the theme and the formula —conflict. In these stories, it seemed a conflict was an absolute prerequisite to a romantic relationship getting underway, and further that, resolving that conflict equated to a happy ending.

Yet, as I looked around, including in my family and the families of my friends, conflict between romantic partners frequently led to divorce—not to 'they lived happily ever after.' As I went through my PhD training in psychology and later had a parent coaching business, conflict in relationships, particularly between the two parents, was often at the heart of the problems for which families sought help. Sadly, this was frequently after a substantial amount of damage had occurred between the parents and the children as well.

As is the case for the characters in a romance novel, our perceptions of conflict can be contradictory. Many people subscribe to the notion that conflict is natural. That it is inevitable; even necessary.

Yet, most of us do not want to admit that conflict is part of our own lives. We see it as negative and something to avoid if possible. We may withdraw from situations that have the potential for conflict, we may give in right away to keep the peace, or we may behave in an aggressive way to put our foot down and try to shut off conflict immediately.

Rule number five: Do not be afraid to face conflicts. Resolving conflict is a part of good communication.

In this chapter, we will unpack the complexities of conflict and how to resolve conflict effectively using mindful communication. We will talk about the causes of conflict, their nature, and the accompanying emotions. We will look at how you can approach conflicts and their resolution with empathy and a problem-solving mindset. Finally, we will spend some time on how to use mindful communication when conflict may arise when interacting with individuals with mental disorders, which comes with its own set of challenges.

What Is Conflict?

Bernard Mayer is a Professor of Dispute Regulation at the Werner Institute housed at Creighton University. He is considered a leader in conflict resolution, having written and practiced extensively for over three decades. Mayer believes conflict happens along three dimensions. These are cognitive (perceptions and beliefs), emotional (feelings), and behavioral (actions).[1]

When we believe or perceive incompatibility between our needs and someone else's, conflict is present for us. We may feel a certain way when there is disagreement. This might be fear, anger, sadness, hopelessness—or any combination. Then, there are actions we take to bring the conflict forward, whether overtly or less directly, to get our needs met.

Another interesting consideration is that while conflict is often known to all parties, the key to Mayer's premise is that conflict does not necessarily take two people. You can experience or believe there is conflict even if the other person does not, or even if the other party is unaware of your interpretation that conflict is present.

- Your co-worker has suddenly become terse with you. You think a conflict is brewing, but she is dealing with the pressures of caring for her elderly mother.
- A new power plant is being built in your community, and you are against it. You begin

writing letters of protest every week to the editor of your local newspaper, yet the CEO of the power plant company never sees them.

Causes Of Conflict

As we have discussed in previous chapters, as humans, we have an extraordinarily strong drive to get our needs met, and as social beings, this is often by other people. At the most basic level, when this does not happen, we experience conflict. There are many reasons we have difficulty getting our needs met.

Poor Communication

Given the premise of this book, it may come as no surprise that poor communication is a primary reason for failing to have our needs met. Whether verbal or nonverbal, spoken or digital, language is the vehicle that allows us to express ourselves about a wide variety of issues.

To a high or low degree, we share our emotions, viewpoints, ideas, and opinions and express the conflicts we are experiencing through language.[2] It is critical, therefore, to use language to accurately communicate information, discuss the conflict, and come to a resolution.

Emotions

Another cause of conflict is our emotions. We may react to situations with conflict because they tap into our emotions and we impulsively react, but it goes further. Our emotions can get in the way of resolving conflict by acting as fuel for the fire.

In previous chapters, we have spent substantial time on emotion regulation because it plays a central role in our successful or unsuccessful interactions with others. Many conflicts might never happen or would not reach a critical breaking point if we could always remain calm and rational.

Mayer takes this a step further: "But of course that is not human nature, even if many of us occasionally pretend that it is. At times emotions seem to be in control of behavior. Sometimes they are also a source of power for disputants. They contribute to the energy, strength, courage, and perseverance that allow people to participate forcefully in conflict." [1]

Identity

Conflict can also occur around issues related to our core identity—our values, history, and culture. When we feel these are under threat, this is often interpreted as an attack. Because these aspects are so integral to us, they are emotionally charged.

Our values, history, and culture are group-defined. Being part of a group gives us a sense of security. If the group is threatened, we personally feel threatened. This can result in conflict with others whom we perceive to be aggressors.[3]

Environment

A final area that is important to recognize as a source of conflict is that of our environment. For example, the likelihood of conflict rises the more we interact with a particular person.[4] At work, more conflicts with co-workers and supervisors are seen when there are more demands, either physical (e.g., shift work, overtime, lack of safety) or psychological (e.g., job insecurity, unclear roles).[5] Chronically stressed couples show breakdowns in their communication, including problem-solving, which is then related to less satisfaction in the relationship.[6]

As we reflect on all the touchpoints for how conflict can arise, the next area to explore is how to resolve conflict in a way that we, and others, get needs satisfactorily met.

De-Escalating Conflict

When we think about being angry or hurt due to conflict, our first response might be, "I just want my day in court." "I need to vent!" "I'm going to get even." However, taking this stance will not lead us to growth and more mature relationships. As we began in this chapter, conflict is likely not something we can always avoid, and it turns out we may not want to.

There is the potential for conflict to arise in any situation or relationship, whether personal, professional, or societal. However, conflict can serve an important role if we understand it as a necessary condition for developing our individual selves, our personal and professional lives, and the community and society.

What does matter is that we a) don't seek and engage in conflict just to assert our power, or b) act destructively in dealing with conflict that comes our way. Working through conflict can promote bonding between individuals. Working through conflicts that arise in social systems helps maintain the group's well-being.

Regardless of the particulars, to successfully reach a lasting resolution to conflict, the first step is to be able to communicate in a calm and peaceful way. This is at the core of how the National Collaborating Centre for Mental Health in the United Kingdom describes de-escalation: "The use of techniques (including verbal and nonverbal communication skills) aimed at defusing anger and averting aggression."[7]

Jill Spielfogel and Curtis McMillen, social work researchers, note that two elements of de-escalation are common across situations. One is the need to reduce our responses to conflicts that are heightened, out of proportion, or harsh. The second element is the need to decrease heightened negative emotions when in the midst of the conflict.[8] If we unpack this, we can better understand the key psychological and emotional factors involved and how they play into our ability to participate successfully in conflict resolution.

We all see the world through our own eyes, and similarly, we look out for ourselves first and foremost—often thinking we are the only rational and reasonable one in the equation.[9] This is where the psychological construct of egocentrism comes into play. It starts early in life when children loudly protest "That's not fair!" and then, as adults, "I only want what I'm due." It's not that the child or you as an adult are wrong—after all, you want to get your needs met. It's about how you go about doing so. This is tied into asserting power and control.

We may be under the impression that the conflict has been resolved once we get our way and are happy. But, of course, the other party is likely to see it differently. Let's say you want your messy teen to keep his room cleaner, and this is causing conflict. You decide to take away his allowance, and not allow him to go out with his friends until he complies. Eventually, he gives in, but once he goes off to college, he becomes even messier as a way to assert his control over his environment, telling his roommates that this is because his mom is an over-reactive 'neat freak' and made his life miserable.

Figure 6.1 Being aggressive during conversations is like a hammer hitting a fragile egg.[10]

The emotional component present in conflict is something almost everyone can relate to, whether personally or as an observer. We might say, "I was so mad I couldn't think straight!" and that happens in a state called "emotional flooding." Our brains are so overloaded and fixated on our feelings that there is less capacity for cognitive processing.[11]

There are also subtle ways that emotions can take over and derail conflict resolution. One is due to our past experiences. When we have unresolved conflict, this can trigger us and ramp up our emotional responses more quickly and to a higher degree than the current situation might warrant. For example, if a person or situation reminds you of another person or situation where you could not resolve a conflict, you may bring those feelings into the current conflict, even if they are not relevant to the present event.

Another way emotions can creep in is if you hold biases toward a certain group. When you encounter an individual from that group, you may bring your negative feelings into the interaction without consciously acknowledging this is happening.

Why Is De-Escalation Important?

De-escalation is not the equivalent of conflict resolution but rather a prerequisite. When tensions escalate, there is a greater chance of harm, both physically and psychologically, to us, others, and property. Escalation is triggered by miscommunication when we perceive a threat, don't trust the other party, or are in the throes of high negative emotion.

When we address conflict with well-conceived strategies, we manage escalation more effectively and can position ourselves for conflict resolution. Next, we discuss such strategies.

Strategies For Conflict Resolution

Because conflict is something we ourselves are intimately involved in as an active party, it has higher stakes attached. More of our identity is involved. We might be at risk of losing an important relationship. We might get fired. We might get assaulted.

Let's take note of what we are trying to achieve when we choose and implement a strategy for conflict resolution. The simplest way to describe this is to think of it as seeking a 'win-win' solution. This helps everyone feel satisfied that their needs are being met and that relationships are preserved through trust, respect, and understanding. Not only will this benefit the process of resolving the current conflict, but it can also make future conflicts less likely to escalate and be damaging.

Active And Compassionate Listening

Active listening allows individuals to feel heard and valued, leading to a reduction in hostility. Active listening has been discussed as a recurring theme in this book on mindful communication, and it is included here for good reason. It has been applied in a plethora of situations, including parent-child interactions, marriage counseling, business management, hostage negotiation, international peacemaking, and more. Incidentally, international peacemaking, in particular, makes use of the nonviolent communication approach developed and used by Marshall Rosenberg, which we introduced at the beginning of the book.[12]

Related to active listening is compassionate listening. The hallmark of compassionate listening is empathy. Putting ourselves in someone else's shoes and seeing the world from their perspective can be challenging.[13] Remember, we have to be able to overcome and put our natural egocentrism to the side. We must be able to listen beyond just the words our communication partner is using. We are listening for their feelings, what values they hold dear, and even what they don't say.

I encourage you to revisit the sections where we have explored active listening, but here are a few particularly important techniques for practicing active, compassionate listening in conflict resolution.

- Demonstrate your empathy by acknowledging the feelings and perspectives of the other party.
- Share back that you have heard what they are feeling and that you validate these.
- Refrain from engaging in blame, criticism, and personal attacks, as this will just alienate the other person.

Managing Emotions

One of the biggest challenges is staying calm and composed during heated conflicts. Here is where techniques for emotion regulation can be your saving grace.

- Ask yourself why you are feeling such strong negative emotions. What is it about the situation that makes you angry, sad, or alarmed for instance? Try to bring the thinking side of your brain to the table.
- When you get emotionally upset and can feel your body tense, do deep breathing.
- Give yourself a pep talk. Tell yourself that you can handle the situation calmly and that you are looking for a win-win solution, even if it might take a while.
- Take a break if things are getting too intense. For example, if you find your heart is racing or your voice is rising, and you can't get this under control, call a time-out. Collect your thoughts and return to the conversation when you feel composed.

A Special Note About Anger

Anger is the most common emotional companion you will likely have in conflict. While it is important to stay calm, this does not mean suppressing your feelings of anger. Instead, we must acknowledge that we feel angry and express this emotion in constructive ways.

- Tell the other person what specific behavior or situation makes you feel angry. Rather than, "You make me so mad. You're such a jerk around my friends!" try, "I get really angry when you make inappropriate comments to my friends just to see their reaction. I feel like you don't respect me or them."

- Be assertive. Standing up for yourself is not aggression. It is assertiveness. Be respectful and calm but express your needs nonconfrontationally, verbally, and with your body language.
- If you find that you are engaged in conflict repeatedly due to your feelings of anger and it is causing substantial problems for you with your family and friends, at work, school, or in the community, you may wish to seek support from a professional.

Reframing

We covered cognitive reappraisal in an earlier chapter. What is happening is we are reframing the way we see an event, a situation, or another person. For many situations where conflict arises, there is a fundamental perspective we bring with us. This is particularly true for our identity, where we have a well-established opinion about how the world should work, how things should be done, about right and wrong.

Kaufman, Elliott, and Shmueli are researchers in consensus building and negotiation. A 'frame' is how we all use scripts to make sense of the world, especially complex information. Frames are valuable due to this. Otherwise, every time we encounter the same situation or event, we would be figuring everything out, including how we feel and should behave.[14] That would be exhausting, to say the least!

However, the authors note (as do others in this field) that these frames can make conflict intractable, meaning very hard to manage and resolve. This is because these frames are deep-seated and built on not just our experiences but our values, beliefs, and history—not things we are likely to let go of easily! Reframing, then, while it takes concerted effort, is an important strategy for conflict resolution.

Figure 6. 2 People in conflict with text about values, beliefs, history.[15]

In resolving conflict, reframing includes but goes beyond empathy. It brings in efforts to find a solution through negotiation and problem-solving. Here are some ways to practice reframing.

Share Perspectives

Come together to give each party a chance to fully share their perspective: what everyone is thinking and feeling, their pressing concerns, and their sought-after needs. This must be done with respect and with compassionate listening. Through this exercise, the parties in conflict often find that tension and hostility dissipate—at least enough to proceed toward resolution.

Find Common Ground

One way to resolve a conflict is to find places where there is agreement. For example, parents in conflict may agree they want to stop fighting in front of their kids. Your co-worker and you may both acknowledge that landing that big client is what you both want. Two sides who are split on what kind of commerce should come into your town can agree that economic growth is the goal.

When common ground is recognized and acknowledged, the parties seem more like one another than only different and can better relate. This opens the door for resolving conflict.

Focus On Solutions

These solutions should be attractive to all parties. This may mean brainstorming and putting many ideas on the table to be discussed, dissected, and altered until that win-win solution emerges. It will be the one that is considerate of all parties, equitable, and does not mean 'you win, I lose' or vice versa.

When It's Okay To Avoid

We cannot always control a situation, but we can make some choices about our personal environment or our reactions to what occurs. There are times when it is advisable to avoid conflict. It just isn't going to result in a positive outcome.

For example:

- You have a colleague who is always trying to start an argument with you. No matter how often you try to interact with him using conflict resolution techniques, he seems to relish the drama. Only interact with him as necessary. If he is at one end of the table in the conference room, choose the opposite end.
- Your two-year-old is constantly saying, "No! Me do it." Rather than get into a battle of wills with a toddler, recognize she is in the stage of autonomy versus doubt. Give her opportunities to do things for herself, even if it's not to your standards.
- It's rush hour on the freeway, and for some reason, another driver seems to have targeted

you in road rage. Stay calm and take the next exit. By the time you get back on, they will be well ahead.

Threat Of Conflict And Mental Disorder

The rates of mental illness among the general population means that you may come into contact with someone who has a mental disorder. There are conditions where individuals are more prone to engage in conflict due to impaired cognitive functioning and their inability to regulate their emotions

While there are some disorders where conflict is more likely, the risk may be lower than some people think. There is greater public awareness of mental health disorders such as depression and anxiety where the general public understands there is less likelihood of violence.

However, there are conditions where individuals are more prone to engage in conflict. These include schizophrenia, bipolar conduct, and oppositional disorder, dementia, and post-traumatic stress disorder.[16] [17] People with these conditions share the characteristic of impaired functioning. Often this is related to the inability to control their thoughts, emotions, or behavior, which frequently disrupts their relationships. Something important to know is that substance use, either illicit drugs or alcohol, has been found to bring conflict even more front and center for people with mental illness.[16]

There is one more mental health condition to cover, and that is narcissistic personality disorder. We often use this as a kind of lay term, but it is a recognized mental health condition. Such individuals over inflate their sense of importance. They need a great deal of attention and admiration. They are mired in egocentrism. In actuality, they are insecure and lack confidence.

It is a challenge to have a mutual and equitable relationship with them because a narcissist has a great deal of difficulty caring about or even understanding the perspective or feelings of others. When they are not getting attention or are criticized, they can become quite upset, feeling substantial hostility and even going into a rage.[18] It isn't hard then to see how they would regularly be in conflict with others.

Overall, people with mental disorders face stigma. They can be treated less humanely, exacerbating the potential conflict situation. If you have to interact with someone who you know or suspect is dealing with a serious mental health condition, here are some strategies.

- Use active listening. Be compassionate, nonjudgmental, and respectful.
- Resolving the conflict in a way that is a 'win-win' for everyone is not always the goal, as it may not be as possible. Instead, it is more important to keep the conflict from escalating. To do so, you may have to just find a compromise.

- Be aware of physical and privacy boundaries as many people with mental health issues don't want to openly discuss their condition or may feel threatened when they feel their personal space is 'invaded.'
- Educate yourself about the condition and how best to support the individual. This is particularly crucial if you have anyone close to you that you interact with regularly who has a mental disorder.
- Be prepared for a crisis if you may be called upon to intervene by having a plan. It is much harder to know what to do on the spur of the moment when things are heated.

By being aware, informed, and prepared you will be better positioned to deal with conflict that may arise when you interact with someone with a mental illness.

We have covered many aspects of conflict. What conflict is, why it arises, and how to mindfully and peacefully engage in conflict resolution. Let's bring this together next.

Putting It All Together

Let's look at a scenario that shows a conflict situation and how it can be resolved using many of the techniques we have discussed.

JoAnne and Timothy are adult siblings whose parents recently passed away. They are now dealing with the division of the estate. JoAnne feels the will is unfair and favors Timothy, as he is the son, while Timothy believes the will reflects their parents' wishes and should be respected.

Their discussions have deteriorated over the past few months and have become shouting matches. This is so upsetting to both of them that they are now on the verge of not speaking. However, this isn't something the siblings can walk away from. They know they have to do something soon to settle the estate.

JoAnne seeks advice from her maternal uncle. He reminds JoAnne of how close she and Timothy were growing up, and still are. He shares his view that their parents would be very disappointed to know the situation, and their relationship has come to this. JoAnne feels herself softening, thinking about her close relationship with her brother and parents. She invites Timothy to a weekend away to try to work this out.

At the resort, JoAnne and Timothy can feel themselves relaxing. As they walk on the beach and then sit poolside, they allow each other to express their feelings and concerns without interruption. JoAnne listens to Timothy's perspective on the will, and Timothy listens to JoAnne's feelings of unfairness. JoAnne empathizes with Timothy's grief over their parents' passing and the importance of honoring their wishes. Timothy empathizes with JoAnne's feelings of injustice and loss.

They even talk about old times and laugh—something they were beginning to think was impossible. This bonding helps them focus more on finding a solution that works for them both. Timothy and JoAnne make a plan to meet with a mediator to help them understand the legal aspects of the will and explore possible solutions that are fair to both parties.

Before leaving the resort, JoAnne and Timothy work together on a set of ground rules, including that they will communicate openly and honestly, and not blame nor criticize. If they fall back into heated discussions, they agree they will take a short break until they both feel calmer.

Two months later, the sister and brother reach a resolution regarding their parents' will. They've decided to divide certain assets differently to address JoAnne's concerns while still honoring their parents' wishes, which are particularly important to Timothy. This outcome allows them to move forward with the estate settlement process and strengthens their relationship.

Action Steps

To reach positive resolutions to conflicts in your life, here are some steps for you to take drawn from this chapter:

• *Reflect.* Taking quiet time to understand the causes, triggers, and drivers of the common conflicts you find yourself engaged in, such as poor communication, emotions, identity, and environment, can increase your self-awareness.

• *Practice.* As with any skill, de-escalating conflict with strategies takes practice. As you deal with conflict, call on the active and compassionate listening techniques, managing your emotions, reframing the situation to see the perspective of others, what you have in common, and how to find the best solution for all.

• *Control Environment.* By avoiding certain situations or people who are not key to your life, you can reduce the opportunity for conflict. With those close to you, don't fall into the trap of thinking everything is a power struggle—in other words, don't necessarily sweat the small stuff.

Chapter Summary

Ultimately, conflict resolution requires courage—but not physical courage. It is the courage to be willing to resolve the inevitable conflicts in life with peace and harmony. That takes work, but the rewards are immense! We have discussed quite a lot in this chapter on conflict and resolution. Let's look at the key lessons.

- Conflict arises when our needs are not met. While this may sound simplistic, it is complex because as human beings we are complex.
- Our interests, values, or desires may be at odds with someone else's, which triggers feelings of

conflict for us, even if they do not know we are experiencing it.

- While conflict is often viewed negatively, it can promote growth and understanding if approached through this perspective.
- The ability to use mindful communication is essential. We share our feelings and listen to understand the feelings of others openly and respectfully.
- Communication, and particularly dialogue, is a vital mechanism for preventing and resolving conflict in ways where everyone wins.

In the next chapter, we will explore self-reflection and introspection. We will look at developing self-awareness and self-expression through strategies for managing internal communication.

7

WHY TALKING TO YOURSELF IS NOT A BAD THING

HOW INWARD DIALOGUES PREPARE YOU FOR OUTWARD CONVERSATIONS

Our ability to communicate is not just outwardly with others. According to research, we conservatively spend 25% of our waking lives engaged in inner speech.[1] Deducting eight hours for sleeping means that in the remaining 16 hours, four are devoted exclusively to dialogue that happens only in our mind just for us to "hear." This is a substantial commitment of our personal resources!

Self-communication, therefore, plays an enormous part in our human experience. Our dialogue with ourselves can serve many purposes, but first and foremost, it is related to awareness of the self. Our consciousness is tightly connected to this running dialogue.

In this chapter, we will explore self-communication and its significance for personal growth through the mechanisms of self-awareness. This then paves the way for introspection, which allows us access to our inner world and self-reflection, which is where we actively learn about who we are.

We will cover the part that mindfulness plays in this journey. We will talk about how self-communication helps us regulate our thoughts, emotions, and behaviors, and how it can help us gain clarity to reach our goals. Like all the skills we have covered to this point, effective self-communication is also a skill. Strategies and techniques can strengthen these and we will offer several to you in practical terms.

The Self

To lay the foundation for this chapter on self-communication, it can be helpful to spend a little time on understanding what the 'self' means as a psychological construct. The self is our sense of our unique identity. It is formed through our cognitive, social, and emotional development and experiences.

The self begins with self-awareness, where we understand that we are separate from others. This early self-awareness occurs over the first two or so years of life. From there, it becomes more sophisticated and takes several forms. One is our self-concept. This is how we perceive ourselves to be—how we might, for instance, describe ourselves to someone. We also have self-esteem. This is how we evaluate ourselves, as humans are inclined to do. Our self-concept tends to be rather stable over time, while our self-esteem can vary based on a particular experience.

- Mark sees himself as someone who makes friends easily. From elementary through high school, this was the case. However, he's starting to wonder if this is still true. He's having trouble making friends now that he's started college.

Mark decides to make more effort to connect with new people rather than waiting for them to do so. By the time the semester ends, Mark has a solid circle of new friends, and once again thinks of himself as someone who can make friends easily.

- Valentina tells people she's a musician because she's been taking piano lessons for years, so technically, that's true, she thinks. However, she hasn't played in public much and sometimes privately feels uncomfortable calling herself a musician.

Her instructors tell her she's got potential, so she takes the plunge, auditions, and gets a gig at a Piano Bar for the summer. It goes so well that Valentina is invited to continue playing there. Now, when she tells people she's a musician, she does so with confidence.

We can see from this discussion and examples that the ability to construct the self is built on being able to think about oneself reflectively—to be self-aware.[2]

Link Between Self-Awareness And Self-Communication

Alain Morin is a psychologist researcher who has extensively studied and written about the connection between self-awareness and self-communication. He lays out a comprehensive model in his paper: "Possible links between self-awareness and inner speech: Theoretical background, underlying mechanisms, and empirical evidence." According to Morin, inner speech is the most important contributor to self-awareness.

This eloquent quote from him gives us insight into why this is the case: "I postulate here that if one does not use inner speech for introspective purposes one will impede self-awareness development; if one does extensively talk to oneself about oneself one will most probably generate a rich and well articulated self-concept."[3]

It is vital to recognize the role that introspection plays because there are different types of self-communication, and they do different 'jobs.'[4] These types typically fall into two categories.

One is self-talk, which is more superficial, such as telling ourselves, "Don't forget to buy milk today" or "Don't bring up Seth's divorce." The other is more complex, such as, "I wonder why I keep sabotaging myself at work by procrastinating and missing deadlines. What can I do to stop this cycle?" or "I was so nervous, but I'm really proud of how well I was able to explain to my tween why she can't start dating yet. I want to use this approach for other difficult conversations with her."

For our purposes, it is the latter type of self-communication, which is also referred to as inner speech or inner dialogue to distinguish it from more simplistic self-talk, on which we will focus. Inner dialogue is where we engage in introspection and self-reflection and tackle the hard issues we face in life. It is where we can grow and progress.

The Role And Benefits Of Self-Reflection

Self-reflection is an adaptive self-focus. It has been associated with less depression, increased feelings of happiness, clearer self-knowledge, and better self-regulation.[5] For example, as we saw in the previous chapter on conflict resolution, we often cannot properly process our own thoughts when we are in the midst of high emotions or immersed in a very charged situation.

This is where the power of self-reflection as we communicate with ourselves comes to assist us. We might say, "When I took a step back…" "Now that I've had time to think about it…" "Upon reflection…" and so on..

Figure 7.1 A woman reflects while looking at a peaceful scene.[6]

This indicates that we have allowed some distance from the event or situation so that we can engage in inner dialogue. We can ask ourselves the questions, "What happened?" "Why?" "How do I feel about my response?" "Is this who I am?" "What could I do next time for a better outcome?"

Self-reflection is directing one's mind to oneself to learn and grow. However, it can, at times, get messy.

Psychologist researchers Leontiev and Salikhova liken it to any other group discussion. Many voices bring varying memories, perspectives, beliefs, and agendas that represent a variety of roles in life (e.g., romantic partner, parent, child, sibling, boss, employee, friend, community member, and so forth).[7] There is a need to bring each of your sub-selves together on the same page, fully explore all perspectives and voices, and then reach a common goal that is in your overall best interest.

While all have value and should be heard, there is one voice that represents a type of self-reflection that is detrimental. This is *rumination*. Rumination is a type of inner dialogue that gets stuck, usually in the negative. It causes us to repeat the same scenarios over and over without resolution. Rumination has been linked to depression and anxiety.[5] [8]

To break this cycle, we have to be somewhat self-detached or objective. Psychologists refer to this as de-centering.[3] [4] [5] We have to distance ourselves to some degree from all the negative thoughts and emotions. Telling yourself, "I'm so dumb," "I will always be a failure," "No wonder no one likes me," and so on, is not constructive and not accurate.

Not that you should never admit your weaknesses; in fact, that is crucial. You just do not need to judge yourself so harshly when doing so. By practicing self-reflection that is based on more accurate and constructive means, you can harness an enormous number of benefits. We take a look at these next.

Increased Self-Awareness

By reflecting in a thoughtful manner on our experiences and exploring the reasons that drive our motives and actions, we can acknowledge our weaknesses, but also recognize our strengths. One area that we can all likely improve upon is emotional regulation. As we explore the foundations for our emotional reactions to others, situations, and events, we are better able to name them, explain them, and then manage them.

Compassion

When we practice self-reflection and introspection with kindness toward ourselves, we are able to accept that we are not perfect but know there is great value in trying to be a better version of ourselves. We learn that we can trust ourselves to be respectful in our self-communication. In previous chapters, we discussed how respect and being nonjudgmental strengthens relationships with others. It applies equally to our relationship with ourselves.

Conflict Resolution

This leads to the next benefit and dovetails with the previous chapter. Introspection can help us see the role we play in conflicts we experience. Self-reflection allows a safe place to reflect on how we might better resolve the conflict. We can play out a number of scenarios and ask ourselves how each might work or where we could improve. You don't have to worry about putting your foot in your mouth when it is done within the safety of your inner dialogue!

Clarification

When we are able to cut through the noise of our negative self's voice, we can better reflect on what truly matters—our core values. It is frequently what we want to accomplish in the short- and long-term. When we engage in systematic and thoughtful self-reflection, we can make a more realistic plan to achieve these goals. Not just, "I hate my boss. I want to work for myself," but rather, "If I started my own business, what would that look like? How can I begin to take steps toward this goal? What am I most afraid of?" and then think it through thoroughly.

Decision-Making

Introspection and self-reflection give you the time and space to consider your options and the possible outcomes. As you then try out these decisions in your external life, you gain additional information that can be rolled into and reflected upon. This positive cycle will help you move toward making better decisions and aid you in reaching your goals, regardless of how simple or complex they may be. A goal might be rather straightforward and somewhat simplistic, such as getting healthier, or it might be rather circuitous and complex, like changing your faith.

All these benefits have one commonality—they allow us to identify the areas where we need and want to grow and mature. We become more intentional. We become our more authentic selves. We experience a better sense of well-being.

Mindfulness And Self-Communication

An exciting area that researchers have more recently explored is the relationship between inner speech/dialogue and mindfulness. This interest in the role of mindfulness in inner dialogue frequently revolves around several key elements: self-awareness, self-regulation, and being nonjudgmental toward the self.

The idea is that mindfulness can facilitate self-concept clarity (you will recall that self-concept is how we perceive ourselves to be), which permits us to formulate more realistic plans. Such plans make it more likely we can achieve our goals.[8]

In reviewing the literature and discussing their research findings, psychologists Racy and Morin relate the findings that mindfulness is associated with more positive self-talk and less self-criticism. Further, mindful awareness is an active state, and the authors propose that this supports more internal activity, which is verbalized and self-directed. Mindful acceptance, on the other hand, is related to decreasing or quieting any inner speech that is judgmental and self-critical.[8]

Both mindful awareness and mindful acceptance are important for complex human experiences. Being able to plan long-term, perform under pressure, appropriately process threatening emotions like shame and guilt, cooperate with others, and so on means we have to be open to deeply reflecting in order to better understand ourselves and the control we can have over these experiences. We have to be willing to have the hard conversations—with ourselves. Mindfulness is one powerful way to achieve this.

Strategies For Effective Self-Communication

As we prepare to explore strategies for effective self-communication, let's revisit some of the core tenets of mindfulness. Practicing these techniques through this lens will give them additional fuel to be more meaningful and useful. Recall the five components that make up mindfulness:

- Acting with awareness
- Observing
- Nonjudging
- Nonreacting
- Describing[9]

Self-communication, being inner dialogue, is based on the verbal, on language. Therefore, the strategies I will share with you have this at their core.

Questions

A great place to start is to answer questions about yourself. This can be particularly powerful if you have little experience 'defining' who you are. One set I like is from Alex Kingman, who is an attachment-style researcher and mental health advocate. His website provides "How Well Do You Know Yourself? The Question Game" from his forthcoming book and covers a wide variety of areas, such as

- How much you like yourself
- What you are passionate about
- How happy you are
- Your future goals
- Your strengths and weaknesses
- Who you admire

You can find the Question Game at "How Well Do You Know Yourself: The Question Game" [10]

<u>Journal Writing</u>

There is a reason that journaling makes the list of strategies for self-reflection and introspection. Hensley and Munn are educators who discuss the research behind reflective journaling. They note that reflective journaling, as an active and focused mental process, is a powerful tool for self-regulation. It can bring focus to past experiences so that meaning can be extracted and problem-solving can be facilitated.[11]

However, it can be challenging when faced with a blank piece of paper, especially if you have not done such journaling in the past. Further, you have a goal in mind to better know yourself and improve your self-communication. A stream of thoughts about whatever pops into your mind may not get you to this goal. You can purchase journals with prompts, but you can also find many online resources.

The Positive Psychology website has a great article on introspection and self-reflection written by Courtney

Ackerman, MA, and reviewed by Tiffany Millacci, PhD, titled "87 Self-Reflection Questions for Introspection [+Exercises]." In addition to questions similar to the previous resource, as well as several self-examination exercises for you to engage with, there are some excellent journal prompts, such as

- What things would you do if you loved yourself unconditionally? How can you act on these things, even if you're not yet able to love yourself unconditionally?
- Name what is enough for you.
- Write a list of questions to which you urgently need answers.

There is also a set of worksheets covering areas such as talents, traits/qualities, values, perception, accomplishments, reflection, and finish the sentence prompts.[12]

Another excellent source for journal prompts can be found on the PsychCentral website in the post titled "Ready, Set, Journal! 64 Journaling Prompts for Self-Discovery," written by Crystal Rayple who has written for Healthline and GoodTherapy and reviewed by Jacquelyn Johnson, PsyD.

Areas covered in the prompts are:

- Love and relationships
- Work and career

- Self-reflection
- Uncomfortable emotions
- Living your best life
- Personal growth and life goals[13]

Poetry

Humans have used poetry and verse for millennia to express our thoughts and emotions about ourselves. You may find that this form of writing works for you to better understand who you are, how you feel about yourself, and your place in the world. If you are unfamiliar with or uncomfortable writing poetry, a great way to dip your toe in the water is to read the poetry of others.

The website PickMeUpPoetry is an independent publishing organization that aims to bring creative voices to the public through a poetic lens. They have a nice collection of self-reflection/introspection poems from well-known and respected poets such as T.S. Eliot, Walt Whitman, William Wordsworth, and Kathleen Raine.[14]

Once you are ready to try your hand at writing poetry, resources for beginners such as MasterClass on "11 Rules for Writing Good Poetry"[15] and "How to Start Writing Poetry (For Beginners)"[16] from Wallflower Journal can be helpful. I particularly like this second one because it encourages the beginner to let go of judgment and discover what ignites creativity.

Creating Self-Affirmations

Self-affirmations are positive statements that help you reduce negative thoughts and replace them with positive ones. Research shows affirmations can be useful for breaking the cycle of rumination, lowering stress, and increasing resilience— the capacity to bounce back from adversity.[17]

Self-affirmations can help you feel better about yourself (your self-esteem—which, to remind you, is how you evaluate yourself) and increase your self-confidence. They can serve as reminders about what you want to accomplish as well.

Affirmations are not the phrases we see on signs we are encouraged to buy for home décor, like "Live, Laugh, Love" or "Be Grateful." Self-affirmations to help you on your path to deeply understanding yourself are a form of self-communication that emerge after much reflection and introspection. They must be personal and meaningful to you. They come from your heart and your mind. They represent you uniquely. But that said, they will change as you do!

The website MindTools frames their work in research and has a good set of ideas for creating your self-affirmations. These include:

- Concentrate on an area(s) you'd like to change in your life.
- Make the affirmation something that is realistic and achievable.

- Hone in on the feelings, beliefs, and thoughts that are most bothering you.
- Write in the present tense to capture the essence of the affirmation already happening.
- Don't shy away from giving the affirmations emotional heft.[18]

Unplug

In today's world, we have access to a plethora of technology-based activities 24/7. From games to reading the news to watching videos to texting, the list goes on. While it may seem a benefit in that we never get 'bored,' the downside is that we reduce the opportunity to be alone with our own thoughts—to engage in self-reflection and introspection.

This can impede our ability to develop and grow as a person. For example, psychologists Sarah Diefenbach and Kim Borrmann found that among young adults, as the amount of time spent using their smartphones increased, there was a decrease in self-insight, that is, a clear understanding of their thoughts, feelings, and actions.[19]

Therefore, a final strategy is that interspersed with the dedicated time and effort spent engaging in specific activities such as questions, journaling, and so on, that you have quiet, uninterrupted time to process and gain personal insights. You may, for instance, not look at your phone for the first few minutes upon waking or before going to sleep, take a walk and resist the urge to listen to music, or as you garden, forgo that podcast occasionally.

For me, drinking my morning coffee and cuddling with my sweet senior cat is a no-technology time. I use this time for self-reflection, and she uses it for getting pets. It sets us both up for a better day!

Let's close this section on strategies by looking at an example journal entry based on self-reflection and introspection.

Today at work, I dismissed one of my co-worker's ideas quickly without weighing the pros and cons. I spent time thinking about why on my drive home. I had to admit that she is seen as a "rising star," while I have been there for over a decade without a promotion. I realize I am insecure, maybe even jealous. By responding as I did, I was trying to shut her down and make her look incompetent and using my seniority, such as it is, to do so.

Thinking back over the past few months, I can recall several times I did this with co-workers. This isn't who I want to be. I want to be a member of the team, who supports and is supported, where we all are valued and can be heard fairly. I know I have work to do on this, but I'm committed to improving my communication and coming to terms with where I am in my career. I'll accept that, or I will need to make a plan to move on from this company. Either way, I need to be a more considerate colleague.

Figure 7.2 Journaling is one of the ways to achieve mindfulness that helps with improving communication skills.[20]

Action Steps

Self-communication can be very challenging. It can, in some instances, seem rather threatening if we are not used to self-reflection and introspection. Yet, as discussed, the benefits are compelling. Here are some action steps for you to follow to enjoy these benefits:

- As you engage in inner dialogue, allow each part of yourself a chance to speak. Be respectful to them, but do not allow the rumination voice to take charge and run the show.
- Remind yourself that you are in a safe space in your mind. Here, you can play out any number

of scenarios, try out various solutions, change your mind, and so forth without the same consequences as in the external world.

- As you engage in self-communication, work to do so in the spirit of mindfulness, being aware of your thoughts and emotions, and observing these without judgment and overreacting, and then describing them verbally to yourself.
- Finally, make a commitment to dedicate time to implementing some of the strategies shared here, with a particular commitment to giving yourself time and space to think introspectively.

Chapter Summary

In this chapter, we explored the importance of self-communication in understanding yourself. By fully harnessing the power of inner dialogue with a focus on self-reflection and introspection, you can experience much more substantial personal growth. Here are some key takeaways for you:

- Self-awareness is the foundation as this is how we develop our sense of self with our self-concept of how we see ourselves and our self-esteem of how we evaluate ourselves.
- Inner dialogue is the goal as differentiated from self-talk. Inner dialogue is a deeper form of self-communication used for reflection and

introspection, whereas self-talk is more superficial.

- The benefits of self-reflection and introspection are far-reaching and include increased self-compassion, conflict resolution, goal clarification, and decision-making.
- Mindfulness can enhance self-communication by promoting self-awareness, self-regulation, and nonjudgmental self-acceptance.

In the next chapter, we will return to relationships with others—this time with family and friends. We will look at why and how such relationships are vital for our well-being and explore how to nurture and enhance connections to maintain healthy relationships.

8

NURTURING RELATIONSHIPS IRL

HOW TO SPEAK BETTER TO BUILD UP
RELATIONSHIPS WITH YOUR INNER CIRCLE,
INSTEAD OF TEARING THEM DOWN

I once heard an old Celtic song with the line, "She was fairer than money." I have often reflected on this, especially when I think about my own daughter. To me, it conveys that when we have an extraordinarily deep connection with another person, this transcends the ordinary, even when that ordinary is itself powerful, like money.

In this chapter, we turn our attention to the relationships that most influence our sense of well-being for humans—our family and friends. We will look at how this impacts our well-being, the dynamics of these personal relationships, and how to use mindful communication to resolve conflict and nurture intimacy and trust.

Personal Relationships And Well-Being

Human beings need intimate relationships to thrive. When I use the term intimate, this does not automatically mean a romantic or sexual closeness, although that is one aspect. Rather an intimate relationship is marked by a close connection with another and includes physical and emotional closeness. We will focus primarily on the latter.

We have many intimate personal relationships within our own nuclear and extended families and in our friend groups. Our emotional well-being is tightly linked to our perception of how available and reliable someone in these close relationships is for us.[1] Our emotions themselves are what drive us to form these relationships, and they are what drive us to keep them going.

How we interact with and communicate with our intimate partners is colored by our emotions. Therefore, our emotional well-being is protected and elevated when we have positive, healthy, close personal relationships. Conversely, our well-being suffers when we are in intimate relationships defined by emotional distance, insecurity, or conflict.

An element that differentiates intimate relationships from those less personal is emotional interdependence.[2] This is when our feelings are intertwined, related, or dependent on the feelings of another. We may experience the other person's emotions deeply—we feel empathy. This frequently goes further and affects how we internally feel —we experience emotion transmission.

There are many theories around intimate relationships and their importance for our well-being, but one that is always brought forward is attachment theory. Let's take a brief look as it will give you a good foundation for understanding the link between attachment and the health of a relationship.

Psychologist John Bowlby's attachment theory is built on the premise that humans are driven to be close to significant others. This begins with our parents and early caregivers, then spreads and continues in our adult relationships.[3]

The basic mechanism for attachment is that when our needs are met, we experience secure attachment. We feel safe and happy. We feel accepted and grateful. We experience love and joy. However, if our needs are not met or are met inconsistently so that we never quite know where we stand, we experience insecure attachment. We are more likely to feel anxious and unhappy. We experience fear of rejection and despair. We feel frustration, anger, and humiliation. While such negative feelings are normal to us as human beings and will inevitably be a part of any close relationship, the difference lies in their intensity and longevity—and how we manage them.

Having secure, positive, and healthy personal connections is primarily a result of spending quality time together and engaging in effective communication. This builds us up personally. It also builds a support network of people to help us in times of trouble and to celebrate us in times of triumph.

All the information and insights we have discussed thus far on effective communication apply to our personal relationships. But as we look at intimate relationships, the situation has higher stakes. For instance, you can much more easily walk away from a deteriorating relationship with a co-worker or your dentist than with your spouse or child.

In our intimate relationships, we have to work harder because we have to negotiate emotional experiences that make us more vulnerable, such as feeling hurt, angry, sad, or disappointed. If we cannot traverse these wisely, we can find ourselves in patterns that destroy closeness. This could be demanding, withdrawing, blaming, or escalating conflict.

Psychologists Karen Wachs and James Cordova found that mindfulness positively impacts the health of intimate relationships. Specifically referring to 'mindful relating' as being open and receptive with attention to the present moment, this supports an inclination to approach a person and build a relationship rather than avoid. Approaching promotes a healthier manner of responding. Further, through practicing mindfulness, we become more able to effectively identify, manage, and communicate emotions, even those that are negative.[4]

Let's look at some practical ways you can nurture close bonds with family and friends through mindful relating and communication:

<u>Use Active Listening</u>. Give your full attention, ask questions to clarify, and process and repeat back. Remember to use "I" statements and avoid blaming or rehashing the past.

<u>Practice Gratitude</u>. Let the people you are closest to know that you appreciate them. This can be as simple as saying "thank you" and "you're welcome" or it can be more elaborate, such as treating them to a special meal or letting them choose the weekend activity. You can, of course, splash out but this isn't necessary to practice gratitude.

<u>Make Time</u>. Life can get very hectic. It's helpful to schedule quality time on your calendar. Find a time when you can connect without lots of distractions. Choose activities that you both enjoy. Resist letting technology get in the way of time better spent having meaningful conversations. Such shared activities are a powerful way to bond. And you'll have some amazing memories!

Figure 8.1 Friends spending time riding bikes as a way to grow their relationship.[5]

Dynamics Of Personal Relationships

Dynamics in relationships are made up of complex patterns. Dynamics bring together our thoughts, emotions, and communication styles. They culminate in repeated behaviors or actions as we interact with the other party in a particular relationship.

Close relationships, in general, have common dynamics. All intimate relationships are a balancing act between dependence and independence. We deeply desire connection and belonging, yet we do not want to be controlled or lose ourselves in the process. We also bring our personal attributes into the mix of dynamics. These are our external experiences, such as our upbringing and previous relationships, and our internal properties, such as intellect, skills, and personality.[6]

Many of these dynamics can play out differently depending on the particular intimate relationship, and the stage of the relationship. Let's look at some of the most common intimate relationships.

<u>Romantic</u>

In romantic relationships, it is not unusual for gendered roles and their subsequent dynamics to be in place. However, in modern times, skills and personality are more often the deciding factors.

That said, this is a relationship where the dynamics of past relationships can often cast a long shadow, for better or for worse. If one or both partners come from a past relationship where the main form of communication was passive aggressiveness for example, they will most likely bring that into the new relationship. However, if they use effective communication, they have a leg up.

With regard to roles, these may or may not follow a traditional path. In some relationships, the woman handles the money, gets the car serviced, etc., and the man is the primary caregiver for the children, does the cooking, and so on. In others, the couple follows a more traditional path. For instance, the man does only the yard work and the woman only the housework. Same-sex couples can take a more masculine or feminine role.

Alternatively, any couple may be more fluid, either sharing equally in roles or taking them on as interest and time permits. Regardless, depending on the degree each person is, and stays, aligned with the expectations set for the roles will contribute to whether the dynamic is healthy or not.

Parent-Child

We know that the child seeks the closeness and attention of the parent for attachment and this drives the dynamic. The dynamic between a parent and young child is also typically that the parent has more power, or more say, than the child. Much of this is because the parent is raising and teaching the child. With this power comes responsibility and this is played out in the dynamic as well.

For example, a parent is busy washing dishes and their toddler wants attention. The parent tells the child they will play with them in just a few minutes, but the child is struggling to wait and begins to cry. The parent tells the child they will not play with them until they stop crying and wait patiently. The parent, rather than the child, is in charge, so to speak.

We also see the situation where a parent cannot recognize their child as an adult or the adult still behaves like a child when they interact and communicate with their parent. However, as the parent becomes elderly, often the roles are reversed and the adult child becomes the caregiver. The dynamics thus shift. In both cases, if all parties are happy with the situation, the dynamic can be healthy, but if one or both are not, the dynamic is problematic.

<u>Friend</u>

This usually is one of the relationships where the dynamic is more balanced. We have more flexibility over our lifespan to choose our friends. We tend to gravitate to those we 'click with.' This is often because we share a similar communication style.

However, this is not always the case. For example, one friend may constantly seem to need rescuing, and the other friend may be the hero figure. We also see imbalances in the friendship relationship dynamics in childhood and adolescence. Kids who are somewhat desperate to 'fit in' may allow themselves to be taken advantage of, yet fiercely defend their peers if criticized by an adult.

As you think about your personal relationships, it can be useful to explore the dynamics of these relationships to gain insights for cultivating deeper connections. Given the central role of communication in our intimate relationships, let's next look at various communication styles and examine their strengths and weaknesses.

Exploring Communication Styles

<u>Formal Vs. Informal Communication</u>

Formal communication is used in settings where following established protocols and etiquette is expected. For example, a professional work situation, attending a funeral, or meeting a dignitary. It uses polite language, rarely veers off-topic, and has little emotionality. This can be contrasted with informal communication. This style is more relaxed and casual and is typically used among family and friends. It may include humor, slang, or even profanity, and emotions are more freely expressed.

- When we are too formal in our intimate relationships, this can be interpreted as wanting to keep one's distance—making bonding less likely. By using the informal style, our emotions are more freely expressed. We can be relaxed, let our guard down, and show our authentic selves.

Direct Communication Vs. Indirect Communication

People are straightforward and to the point in the direct communication style. Honesty is valued. Thoughts, feelings, and opinions are expressed openly and straightforwardly. This is contrasted with indirect communicators. People who gravitate to this style may use subtle hints, physical gestures, or other nonverbal cues to convey their messages instead of outright stating them.

This is not to say there is no place for nonverbal communication. While indirect communication is marked by someone not conveying what they mean, nonverbal communication is a way to convey meaning without words. Nonverbal communication, such as facial expressions, body language, and tone of voice, plays a significant role in conveying emotions and messages and can accompany direct verbal communication. There is a big difference between someone who walks out of the room whenever you enter because they are mad at you and someone who chooses to sit across the room from you as they share they are angry with you and why.

- The indirect style can sometimes lead to misunderstandings or misinterpretations. Being direct helps the other person have clarity about what we wish to communicate—they don't have to 'read our mind.'

Passive Communication Vs. Assertive Communication

Somewhat related to direct vs indirect communication, people with a passive communication style often avoid confrontation and prioritize not rocking the boat, keeping the peace, or just going along. Assertive communicators, on the other hand, express their needs, thoughts, and feelings clearly and confidently while respecting the rights and the point of view of others. Part of that respect is communicating with empathy, where we feel genuine concern and understanding for the emotions and experiences of the other person in the relationship.

- If we always put the feelings and needs of others above our own, eventually, this will lead to resentment and undermine the closeness we can have with someone. Being assertive is not being aggressive; rather, it is how we get our needs met in a way that helps us be happier—and that makes its way into the relationship dynamic.

Passive-Aggressive Communication

This final style is not contrasted with another but is in its own league because it combines the more destructive styles we discussed above. In passive-aggressive communication, individuals express their dissatisfaction or opposition indirectly, often resorting to sarcasm, subtle insults, or nonverbal cues to convey their feelings. They are not trying to keep the peace, but they may think they are. People who choose this as their main communication style are often confused and unsure of their place in the relationship.

- When we engage in passive-aggressive communication, we will not foster understanding and intimacy because there is a strong sense of mistrust on both sides. The communicator is not confident that they will be accepted if they express their true feelings. The receiver is not confident they will be treated kindly when they say what is on their mind.

In our intimate relationships, we can see that we would want to strive to be informal, direct, and assertive communicators. In this way we can form close bonds with others that can greatly enrich our lives.

Figure 8.2 Friends talking with direct and active engagement promotes bonding and connection.[7]

Parenting With Mindful Expression

While we have many important and close relationships, I want to spend some time specifically on the parent-child relationship. As mentioned above, it comes with a great deal of responsibility. Not only do you have that specific relationship to manage, but you are teaching another human being how to have healthy relationships—all at the same time. This can be a big undertaking!

Mindful parenting incorporates many of the concepts of mindful communication. Larissa Duncan and colleagues offer a mindful parenting model that highlights being fully present, nonjudgmental, and showing empathy.[8] Further, it helps parents practice self-regulation of their emotions. It reduces the impulsivity we may feel when our child does something negative, especially if it is unexpected. This helps alleviate some of the inherent daily stress associated with parenting, which when high, has been found to be associated with parents being more controlling and showing less warmth toward their child.[9]

Mindful parenting also supports making good choices in our parenting. Rather than being reactive, the mindfulness aspect encourages taking time to think and process to come up with the best course of action. Mindful parenting aligns with many of the concepts in the authoritative parenting style, which results in the most secure attachment bond between child and parent.[10] Here, the parent sets appropriate boundaries based on the child's developmental stages. They recognize the child's emotions and show empathy but are not permissive. Children thus feel safe and secure.

Nigela Ahemaitijiang and colleagues conducted an in-depth review of the mindful parenting research and concluded that this approach benefits the parents, children, and the family as a whole. Let's take a look at how you can practice parenting mindfully.[11]

Environment

This is both the physical and the emotional. 'Childproofing' your home is key for safety, but it also helps your child avoid situations where there will be conflict. Rather than always telling your toddler not to play with the expensive and breakable décor on your coffee table, move it until they have better impulse control. Instead of setting a rigid rule that your teenager must do his homework with no music, allow him to show this does not negatively impact his grades.

Communication

Effective communication is a central key to a strong parent-child relationship. Using mindful communication and expression revolves around communicating with empathy to build trust and emotional connection. Using active listening and validating a child's feelings is essential. We may tend to underestimate the deepness with which children experience the world and how big their emotions are. They need patience and acceptance from their parents to express these as their language and emotion regulation skills are still developing. Children can also show their emotions in ways other than just a direct conversation, for example, through art or play.

When my daughter was about three, she started a game with me called "Giraffe," and the main character was a small, rather silly-looking stuffed giraffe. Giraffe got herself into all kinds of scrapes, and I was tasked with being given the part, with my daughter deciding all the scenarios. My daughter took on the persona of 'Kitty.' There was not a stuffed kitty; this was my daughter firsthand. Kitty was the well-behaved one in the relationship. We played "Giraffe" for the next four years. I have to be honest that it was sometimes exhausting, but I watched my daughter work out the conflict between being good and being naughty in an impressive number of variations.

<u>Discipline</u>

By setting up the environment appropriately and using mindful expression, you will preempt situations of conflict, but you will not reduce them all. There will be many times when you will be called on to address inappropriate behavior. Let's first clear up the difference between discipline and punishment. Discipline is about guiding, correcting, and teaching to help children make better choices. Punishment has the air of making a child suffer for infractions.

Punishment is always negative, whereas discipline can use negative and positive reinforcement. Let's look at an example. If a child is allowed to go outside and play after they finish their chores, this is positive reinforcement. They get something positive for a desired behavior. If they finish their chores to avoid having outside playtime taken away, this is negative reinforcement. They avoid something negative by choosing to engage in the desired behavior.

This can seem like splitting hairs, but let's look at the messaging. Which seems more loving? Your child being told, "If you finish your homework, you get to go outside and play," OR "If you don't finish your homework, you can't play outside today." When we can, we want to frame the consequences as positive.

However, one thing to note is that you don't want to give too many extrinsic rewards. This is like a treat such as candy, buying a toy, and that kind of thing. This is not only hard to keep up, but it also sends the message that just feeling good about yourself and your accomplishments isn't enough. Instead, guide your child in their own mindfulness and self-communication exercises.

For example, if your child studies hard and makes a high grade on an exam, ask them how this makes them feel. Help them express this if they are struggling to label and articulate their feelings. Happy, relieved, proud, confident, and so on. Celebrate by sharing the good news with their grandparents. Put the test paper on the fridge. Remind them the next time they feel nervous about an exam that by studying as hard as they have before, they will do well.

Tantrums And Conflicts

Because children are learning self-control and developing language skills, they can have 'meltdowns.' Just as we have discussed that as adults, we are not able to communicate effectively when in the throes of high emotion, this is true for children as well.

The best course of action is to give space to allow emotions to cool down. For younger children, a calm-down corner with their favorite lovey can help them relax. For older children, taking a walk, watching a funny show, or playing a few minutes of their favorite video game can reduce the intensity.

You, too, may need to take a break and have a cup of tea or do some meditation to give yourself time to calm down and think about how you want to approach the situation. This also teaches your child that it is okay to have these feelings and models how to manage them. They can then better understand that emotions must be regulated so that one can think clearly and make good decisions.

<u>Self-Reflection</u>

Continuing with that, self-reflection is a central aspect of mindful parenting. Understanding our own emotions and triggers contributes to more mindful and effective parenting. We will tend to parent as we were parented. If we did not have positive role models in this respect, we would have to work harder to practice mindful parenting and expression with our children.

Using some of the strategies and techniques we have covered in previous chapters can help you in this journey, such as asking yourself questions, journaling, and/or meditating in order to clearly think about the kind of parent you want to be and how to best achieve this goal.

Practicing mindful parenting can create a nurturing and supportive environment for children. Communicating with empathy and active listening fosters children's trust and emotional connection. Positive discipline teaches children to manage their behaviors and have confidence in their abilities.

Resolving Conflicts And Maintaining Healthy Connections

We've covered a bit about resolving conflict throughout the chapter, but in this section, we will expand on this and the information from the chapter on conflict resolution as it applies specifically to intimate relationships. There are myriad reasons for conflict to arise in our closest relationships. Expectations are not met. We have goals that do not match. We shuffle for power and control in the relationship. We may simply be extremely annoyed with the other person's bad habits, from not managing money well to leaving wet towels on the floor.

When these conflicts arise and are unresolved, we can feel our relationship suffering. On top of this, just knowing we need to address the conflict and having anxiety about how well we will communicate as we do so is an added pressure. Psychologists Nickola Overall and James McNulty note that according to relationship therapists, communication around dysfunctional conflict causes the most damage; therefore, communicating effectively is a critical skill that needs to be learned.[12]

Resolving conflict is essential in our relationships with friends and family. Doing so has a transformative impact on our well-being by maintaining healthy and meaningful connections. Otherwise, we stay mired in hostility rather than affection.

Strategies For Conflict Resolution In Intimate Relationships

I invite you to revisit the earlier chapter on conflict resolution for a foundation. In addition, here are some particularly important points to keep in mind in intimate relationships.

1. Identifying the root causes and triggers of conflicts rather than focusing solely on surface-level disagreements is key. Until these are revealed and acknowledged, they will continue to make their way into the relationship. Consider this scenario.

Your best friend since childhood has blown you off three times for going out to dinner. You know she is busy, and you understand that it isn't that she doesn't care about you, but you feel yourself cooling toward her. Each time it happens, this has brought back memories of after your parents divorced and your dad frequently didn't show up to take you out to eat as promised. Sometimes, he would call at the last minute, but often, you would be ready and then wait for hours with no word.

You realize you feel abandoned by your friend just as you did by your dad. You decide to call your friend and tell her how you're feeling. You know it's a bit intense, but you are still surprised when she starts crying on the phone. You tell her you are sorry and didn't mean to upset her so much. She replies that she is the one who is sorry. She shares that she remembers how devastated you were when your dad was a no-show, and she would never want you to feel that way about your relationship with her.

2. Finding common ground and shared goals results in collaboration. This can be very beneficial for resolving conflict as collaboration fosters a sense of unity and strengthens connections. The spirit of collaboration is 'win-win' and as discussed in the conflict resolution chapter, this is the type of solution that will allow all parties to get their needs met. Consider these common situations.

- Where to spend the holidays. Rather than arguing each year, come up with a schedule that alternates in a way that both parties feel good about.
- Whether to spend the tax return on paying off bills or taking a luxurious vacation. Working together to decide which is more important at this time will mean that neither is resentful if their priority is downplayed.
- When your child can start dating. Having honest and open dialogue with your child about this next big step rather than lecturing or setting such strict rules that they see this as being extremely unfair and feel compelled to rebel.

3. Setting and respecting healthy boundaries fosters mutual respect. It can also help prevent misunderstandings from further occurring. Practicing active listening and nonviolent communication is a good

foundation for setting boundaries. Here are some examples of boundaries that you can set to ensure effective and respectful communication during times of conflict.

- Communicating expectations of what you will and will not accept behavior-wise is setting healthy boundaries. These may be very serious, such as substance abuse, physical abuse, gambling, or infidelity. Being clear about these is crucial, which is why the chapter on self-communication is so important. It allows you to know yourself and what matters most to you.
- During discussions, rules such as not yelling, throwing objects, or using profanity are examples of healthy boundaries.
- Sticking to the topic will help you stay on track and within the boundaries of the situation. If you feel it is important to bring up past hurts, make sure they are relevant and that you speak of them specifically regarding the situation at hand. Rather than "You always…" try, "I feel like there is a pattern that whenever I try to talk to you about our finances, you tell me I'm just overreacting. This makes me upset and even uncertain about what I believe is a very important issue for us to resolve."

4. Finally, you are in the midst of a conflict because there has likely been a rift in your relationship with a family

member or friend. This could be rather small-scale but still hurtful, or it could be a major mistake that severely threatens the relationship—either of your making, the making of the other person, or even to which both of you have contributed.

We have a great deal of emotion and needs invested in the people with whom we have the most intimate relationships. It is, therefore, important to acknowledge the power of sincere apologies and forgiveness in healing conflicts. Rebuilding trust and moving forward together is a process. Here are some ways to go about this.

- Be patient. It can take time to process and work through the pain, but if you stay committed, you will be able to do this. That said, it will be a struggle if you are not sure you want to work it out. so it is important that you have the goal that the conflict will end in a peaceful resolution.
- Call on feelings of empathy. Put yourself in the other person's shoes for the frustration, anger, or sadness they are feeling so that you can acknowledge it to the other person. This is powerful for healing.
- Be open to exploring the underlying reasons for the conflict. It may be more on the other person, but it may be you. Being open and receptive to the fact that you have to be forgiven can feel threatening. Just remember, this is an opportunity for you to grow and mature.

As we think about and explore these strategies, it is important to acknowledge that some conflicts within families and friendships are very complex and may be beyond your capacity to deal with them on your own. If this is the case, you may find that seeking professional mediation or counseling is needed.

I want to stress that one of the biggest stumbling blocks can be getting to mediation or counseling in the first place because the other party isn't interested or ready. I encourage you not to let that stop *you* from seeking help. Also, while not always the case, many times, once one person begins to see the benefits, the other person is more willing to participate.

Action Steps

As we reflect on the importance of mindful communication in building strong, close relationships with those who mean the most to us, our family and friends, here are some action steps for you to implement mindful communication to build strong, close relationships and keep them going.

- Make an effort to spend quality time with family and friends, and express your gratitude for them being in your life.
- Consider your communication style. Practice active listening and focus on mutual respect, collaboration, and forgiveness when conflicts arise.

- If you are a parent or have children in your life, implement the mindful parenting approach.
- If communication breaks down and you are unable to handle complex relationships, consider seeking professional help.

Chapter Summary

In this chapter, we explored the importance of intimate relationships for our well-being and how such relationships can be nurtured and strengthened through mindful communication. Here are some key takeaways for you.

- As humans, we need intimate relationships for our emotional well-being. When we feel safe through secure attachment, this lays the lifelong foundation for positive and healthy relationships. Such relationships are marked by emotional closeness and influence our happiness.
- Every relationship has unique dynamics—a complex interaction of thoughts, emotions, and communication styles. Aiming for informal, direct, and assertive communication rather than formal, indirect, passive, or passive-aggressiveness fosters stronger connections.
- Parenting is one of life's most important roles. Mindful parenting emphasizes being fully present, nonjudgmental, showing empathy, and practicing emotional self-regulation for effective

and peaceful parenting. This teaches children healthy emotional expression and conflict resolution so they can have strong relationships, not just with parents but with their friends and family.

- To successfully resolve conflict, it is key to identify the root causes, find common ground, establish healthy boundaries, practice active listening, and do so in a spirit of forgiveness.

In the next chapter, we look at fostering positive communication and collaboration in professional settings to promote a healthy work environment.

9

LET'S MAKE IT WORK AT WORK!

CRACK THE SECRETS TO BEING A MASTER COMMUNICATOR IN THE WORKPLACE

"Must be a team player."

This requirement appears in practically every job posting in every industry. Something so common it's likely not even processed by us, whether we are seeking a position or hiring for one. Yet, we all acknowledge the spirit of being a team player is fundamental to effective communication in the workplace.

This chapter focuses on fostering positive and mindful communication in professional settings and promoting a healthy work environment. We will cover active listening, building productive relationships with colleagues, collaborative teamwork, effective delegation, managing conflicts, and providing and receiving constructive feedback.

Communicating In Professional Environments

Given the staggering nearly 100,000 hours we spend at work over the course of our working life[1], the importance of professional communication cannot be overstated. We spend a significant amount of time with our work colleagues—perhaps even more than with our friends and certain family members!

When workplace communication is effective, it can make working a pleasant and productive experience. When ineffective, it can make that same experience negative and draining. We have likely all experienced both and can vividly recall how we felt or how we currently feel. With effective communication, the team is engaged and motivated. People are on the same page. Trust is high. All of this leads to getting goals met. It's fulfilling.

How does this come about?

Communication, verbally and nonverbally, takes place through many forms in the workplace. We speak in person, over the phone, and more and more through video meetings. A substantial amount of our communication is also written. We write emails, post on messaging boards, send texts, and complete more formal written communications such as performance reviews. All of these are important to consider when we discuss effective communication.

Active Listening

Each type of communication benefits from active listening. Using active listening in the workplace garners all the benefits we discussed each time we covered this technique in previous chapters. Yet, active listening in the workplace carries a few additional benefits.

Accuracy. In business, the stakes can be high if our communication is not accurate. By making sure that messages are stated with clarity, we can decrease errors.

Problem-solving. When everyone is free to express themselves without worrying about being shut down, ideas to tackle problems flow. Everyone's voice is heard to ensure diverse perspectives are incorporated. This allows creativity to come to the forefront.

Efficiency. Active listening means focusing on what our work colleagues think, feel, and plan on doing. This helps projects smoothly move forward. The decision-making process is not mired by miscommunication, or worse, by sabotage because people feel hurt and disenfranchised.

Empathy

Miscommunication is why understanding and empathy matter so much. Empathy is an important component of active listening, yet it can be challenging in a work setting for a few reasons. Melissa Fuller is a communications researcher, and she and her colleagues studied empathy competence through extensive interviews with 35 expert-level communication professionals. In addition to citing research that empathy improves workplace performance, they note that empathy skills are decreasing.

The expert participants shared that increasing one's skills in this area is about going below the surface. As humans, we often feel more than we say, either because we don't trust our listener, or because we have not allowed ourselves to fully process what we are feeling.

This could be because we have a conflict with someone and are avoiding it, or we are competitive to the point where we might not want to have an emotional connection to someone because we would not always do what is in their best interest.[2] Or that, as we discussed in the chapter on biases, we are working with colleagues with whom we cannot, or do not want to, relate.

Yet, we know that a deeper connection with any other person, especially those we spend so much time with such as work colleagues, is needed both for our personal well-being as well as the health of our company, organization, or institution—whether a Fortune 500 company or a small coffee shop.

Let's look at the skills that can help you be a more empathetic listener with your co-workers:

• Active listening, especially giving someone the space to share, paying attention to nonverbal cues, paraphrasing, probing for more or deeper information, and regulating your own emotions.

• Being culturally aware, attending to a propensity to filter through any biases you hold, and having an understanding of the myriad emotions someone could be experiencing.

• Having an attitude of openness to the experiences of others, paying attention to the context in which information is shared, being honest and authentic, and looking for win-win solutions.

Boundaries

Just as we discussed setting boundaries in your intimate relationships, setting boundaries in your professional relationships is critical. Setting boundaries appropriately promotes mutual respect and a healthy work environment.

In the workplace, boundaries can fall into several categories that are relevant to your relationships with colleagues. These may be physical, psychological, or a combination. Physical boundaries may relate to personal space or they may be something like time, especially work-life balance. A psychological relationship may include co-workers expecting you to pick up their slack, having someone else take credit for your work, or gossiping.

Let's look at some common scenarios and how you can set appropriate boundaries in professional relationships.

<u>Physical Boundaries</u>

Our physical boundaries might be tested because we are working in close proximity to others. You may be in a small restaurant kitchen where everyone has to participate in a highly orchestrated dance to avoid collision. You may have a tiny cubicle surrounded by dozens or even hundreds of other people. You may have co-workers who like to come into your space and sit on your desk to chat while you are clearly busy. Here are some strategies for you around setting physical boundaries.

- If you feel your personal space, given the constraints of the job, is being invaded, openly, but respectfully, communicate this. Tell the person, "The kitchen is really intense today. After things calm down, I'm going to go outside and take a walk." "I work better if I have headphones on because the noise in the office is distracting." "I'm not a hugger."
- Personalize your space to give yourself a bit of a sanctuary and comfort.
- Use resources such as quiet common areas or empty conference rooms when you feel overwhelmed.
- Use nonverbal cues such as standing or sitting a bit apart, avoid leaning in or over others and move away if they do so, and take the stairs instead of the elevator.
- There is absolutely no tolerance for crossing physical boundaries, such as someone touching another person without their consent. If this

occurs, you should immediately seek guidance from Human Resources.

Work-Life Boundaries

We live in a world where we can always be connected. I am old enough to remember work before the internet. It is true we sometimes took work home, but we did not have to dread an email or text from a co-worker or boss during non-work hours.

With the internet and mobile devices, we may continue to work at home, or if we work remotely, just keep going. Research shows that we are now working more hours and feel pressure to always be available, which gives us less time for recovery and negatively impacts our well-being.[3]

Figure 9.1 Always working detracts from a healthy work-life balance.[4]

However, that is not work-life balance. In order to strive for this, we have to be willing to set boundaries in the midst of an ever-increasing hustle culture. If we do not, our patience, enthusiasm, motivation, ability to be fully present, and so on, as we work and communicate are severely compromised. In the worst form, we will suffer burnout. Here are some strategies for you to move toward work-life balance.

• Take some time to identify your priorities. For instance, how much time and effort are needed for work, and how much for personal life? Write these down so that you can get comfortable with them in preparation for communicating them to others.

• Learn to say no. Keep in mind setting work-life boundaries will likely mean learning to say no to certain people and requests. If you are clear with yourself about what is your responsibility and what is not, it will be easier when these situations arise.

• Pay attention to time management. If you set a boundary that you will stop work at five, make sure you have set up your day to get the necessary tasks completed. Remember to avoid multi-tasking, as this breaks concentration and can easily derail your schedule.

• Do remain flexible. Even if you put all these other pieces in place, there may be occasional exceptions and you will need to adjust. There is a big difference between a colleague who is in a real crunch and needs help working late to make a quarterly deadline and a co-worker who expects you to help every Friday afternoon because she is chronically in danger of missing weekly deadlines. The former is being a team player; the latter is being taken advantage of.

Mental/Psychological Boundaries

This really taps into the dynamics of relationships. You'll want to remember that relationships are full of emotion, which goes for the ones you have with your colleagues. You have a co-worker who always tries to bring in drama, and you feel yourself getting increasingly angry. You and your partner just landed a contract that keeps the company afloat for another six months and you feel a sense of pride in the work you did together. You experience anxiety every time you are called in to talk about your task list with your boss. The co-worker you've been mentoring was promoted and you feel a sense of happiness.

These relationships will always include a mixture of the positive and negative. You just want to aim for the positive being in the majority. Mindful communication can greatly facilitate this for you. Here are some techniques to help you establish healthy mental and psychological boundaries.

- Use the direct, assertive communication style we discussed in the previous chapter. Practice saying

"No" in your inner dialogue, playing out the pushback you may receive and how you will respond.

- Always be respectful when speaking to or about others regarding their work and performance. You don't want to find yourself defending remarks that are belittling. Focus on the task and what needs to happen in order to accomplish it.
- Limit how involved you get in the personal lives of your co-workers and how much you allow them to know about yours. It's fine to be friendly and chat about your weekend, but think twice about friending on social media or listening to the negativity and oversharing that some people thrive on.

These will set you up to build productive relationships with colleagues, which we turn to next.

Building Productive Relationships With Colleagues

A work environment is usually quite a charged setting. There is much at stake to keep the doors open and the lights on. Tensions can quickly run high. By building productive relationships with colleagues, we are better able to weather these storms, and come out better on the other side. In a relationship with co-workers, there are many moving parts—perceptions, attitudes, beliefs, emotions, and responses. To have a functional work environment, we have to be able to interact with colleagues positively and healthily.

Emotional intelligence in the workplace has been found to foster a work environment that is supportive, collaborative, and productive rather than one that is rigid, hostile, and unproductive.[5] We introduced emotional intelligence earlier in the book, but let's refresh our memory. Emotional intelligence can be thought of as a set of competencies. These include two major components. One is the ability to recognize the emotions and motivations of ourselves and others. The second is to be able to manage these well.

A central skill of an emotionally intelligent person is effective communication. When there is good communication among team members, this reduces misunderstandings in particular. When there are a host of misunderstandings, this can result in poor performance. Why?

People do not know what they are supposed to do. They may feel hurt or angry, believe they are not being supported, and so on. There is poor work division, work is not completed, and deadlines are missed. This not only can derail that immediate work—the report that has to be prepared, the shipment that must go out, the customer that must be served, etc., but can severely undermine motivation.[6] A lack of motivation is another layer that is like a dark cloud hanging over the work that needs to be done, slowing it down as people disengage.

Miscommunication

Sometimes in order to know how to improve something, we need to understand where the problems lie. Edward Brewer and Terence Holmes, professors in communications and business management, offered findings from work in which they conducted communication exercises. A main impetus for their work is that it is common for there to be misunderstandings among team members.

These researchers frame their work in models with various levels that contribute to misunderstandings. For example, one area is awareness. While some people may be aware that there is a misunderstanding, others are not. This could be because they don't pick up on the cues, or because they think that's the way things are supposed to be and don't question it.[6]

Another area is more internal to an individual. It has to do with differences between people, with some wanting to remedy misunderstandings while some blame other team members for the situation or foster misunderstandings intentionally. Finally, there is the nature or makeup of the team as an entity. A major source of misunderstanding is having differing cultural or worldview perspectives.

In their learning exercise, the results of the work by Brewer and Holmes fell into the following categories: coordination (organization and time management), clarity (specificity), cooperation (understanding differing views), and consciousness (awareness).

Strategies To Build Productive Relationships

Let's look at some strategies that tap into these areas so that you can build more productive relationships with your team members.

Consciousness For Awareness

This sets the stage for productive relationships and any strategy or technique that follows. Awareness is more likely when we practice direct and open communication with empathy. Having quick check-ins, more in-depth meetings, and eliciting feedback from the team regularly keeps information flowing and prevents miscommunication and misunderstandings.

However, make sure there is a point to these. We've all seen the memes on "this could have been an email", which is really about people not buying into connection— that's not what we want of course.

Clarity For Specificity

An excellent starting point is active listening. This allows you to practice being fully present and ensuring you understand and are understood. When meetings occur, keep detailed notes with action items and make sure everyone has access. Clear and concrete instructions on a task will help avoid confusion. Unless you are sure everyone is up to speed, avoid too much jargon and acronyms.

Take that extra moment to be precise. One example I can offer from my work with clients in different parts of the world is the date and time. Today at 11:30 a.m. for me in the United States is the day after at 1:30 a.m. for a colleague in Australia. If either of us just asks for a meeting tomorrow morning, the other has to do the mental calculation and then take the time to confirm—that's irritating! Finally, if you work with a diverse group, be particularly sensitive to language barriers.

Coordination For Organization And Time Management

Using shared tools designed for project management supports transparency and accountability. This could be calendars, platforms, data storage and filesharing, notetaking tools, and so on. These can serve as a central repository for tasks, the breakdown of assignments, timelines, and status.

One note about this. There has been an explosion of these tools, and it can be tempting to try the 'new and improved,' but remember there is a cost. People can become weary of having to learn a new system and may not do so efficiently because they are aggravated.

Cooperation For Understanding Different Views

First, everyone must be aware of the goals and the tasks needed to achieve said goals to foster cooperation. Then, embrace creative brainstorming and respectful debate. If you go into these activities without first knowing the parameters of the goals and tasks, valuable time can be wasted, and people can get frustrated and they will shut down.

As you generate ideas, solutions, and approaches, be sure these are not only captured, but they go somewhere. Putting all that energy into such exercises and never seeing them acted upon will put a serious damper on motivation to participate in the future.

On the other hand, when we are all working together in an open and accepting manner, especially to solve a pressing problem, this serves as an opportunity for bonding and fosters a sense of camaraderie. We experience trust. We feel valued. We believe we belong. That is a recipe for a positive, healthy relationship with our co-workers.

Figure 9.2 Cooperative and collaborative team meetings promote positive relationships with co-workers.[7]

A strong, healthy relationship with our co-workers becomes even more important in a team setting, as this is frequently how our work is carried out. We look next at collaborative teamwork.

Collaborative Teamwork

Teams are an interesting phenomenon because while they have commonalities, the way they look can differ. A team can be long-standing or it can be formed for a shorter project. A team can have a clear and designated leader, or the leadership may be rotated or even equally shared.

Regardless of their individual characteristics, there are benefits to teamwork.[8] These include a stronger commitment to work, higher job satisfaction, increased institutional knowledge, better results and outcomes, and overall efficiencies for the organization. Conversely, in teams there is the potential for disadvantages. We discussed misunderstandings, but there can also be outright conflicts.

Effective communication is vital to garnering benefits. Mitra Raappana and Tessa Horila are researchers who study team communication in the workplace. In reviewing the literature in this area, they note that through team communication, roles and rules are constructed. There are dynamics at play. Relationships are formed. Naturally, the more people there are on a team, the more complex these become. This has implications for trust, which is essential for authentic collaboration.[8]

Teams have a great deal to communicate about. They have to figure out what the team needs and how to get those needs met. They have to motivate one another. They have to ensure the work gets planned and executed. The better the communication, the better teams can collaborate to achieve these goals.

You can be an amazing team member, but if your colleagues are not, the team's full potential cannot be realized. Therefore, it is important that the team is open to thinking about and evaluating the health of their communication. Let's look at some strategies that you can use to get your team humming along.

Shared Vision

One of the most powerful strategies is working toward a shared vision and the necessary goals to achieve it. This gives everyone direction and a purpose for the work.

Open communication

This is active listening at its core. Psychological safety for sharing feelings, thoughts, and ideas is essential for trust. A setting where people feel free to put themselves out there, and even make mistakes, typically leads to better solutions.

Embracing Diversity

We are all fortunate to live in a time when we have team members from many different backgrounds with different ways of working and thinking about problems and solutions. Valuing our colleagues' unique strengths and perspectives can be very beneficial for effective collaboration and teamwork as we all push ourselves out of our comfort zones.

Recognizing Team Members

We all want to be given credit when we make a meaningful contribution. While the phrase "there is no I in TEAM" is true, what this should not shut down is individual recognition. Always saying 'we' gives the impression the contribution of a single member is not significant, which is rarely true.

When the hard work of a team member is acknowledged, job satisfaction can skyrocket. This is both for the individual and for the other members as they see that their efforts will be recognized. When it comes to more formal recognition, remember it may be at an individual level. While Carol loves that bunch of balloons for a job well done, Tina would appreciate less attention and a gift card instead.

Making Opportunities

Regular connection is key as we discussed earlier but further, if the team is large, you may need smaller working groups who dig into certain aspects and then come back together with the larger team for presentation, feedback, and tweaking. Be vigilant to ensure that this practice does not result in fractions forming. If it seems this is happening, for the team's health there may need to be a reshuffling of members on the sub-teams.

Professional Development

While we recognize each team member has strengths, these should not be static. Not only will the skills of the team members and the organization increase, but the motivation to improve will as well. Growth on the job can happen in a variety of ways. It will depend on the needs and preferences of the team members. Creating a professional development plan for each person every year is a task worth doing. It may be a course, a book purchase, or perhaps mentorship.

Keep in mind some people get 'mentored' almost as a form of punishment. Effective mentorship instead is a relationship marked by learning where there is a balance between support and challenge for the purpose of helping to guide someone on the path of their choosing.

Delegating

Delegating deserves its own attention. As everyone learns the strengths and interests of the team members, it will be easier to delegate tasks so that work can occur effectively.

Research shows that effective delegation can reduce the workload on others, provide growth and development opportunities to individuals, strengthen the whole team's expertise, and increase the organization's efficiency.[9] It is also associated with better relationships and trust among team members.[10]

Yet, delegation is tricky for many of us because it fundamentally revolves around authority and power. Two things in particular can cause delegating to fail. One is because the expectations are not clear, or we are tasked with something that we do not have the skill to do well. This can occur when a manager selects the wrong task and/or team member for the job. It also happens if we volunteer for something we are not quite up to or we don't speak up when we are given a task well beyond our scope.

The second behavior that can undermine this is micromanaging, where there is supervision and control that is excessive for the situation. Team members that have been delegated to do a task, or are the delegators, must be supported and empowered. Ownership is key, but more critical is the belief that we are trusted to succeed.

Edosa Oviawe works with global rights organizations and lays out why managers struggle to delegate, and just as importantly, why people resist having tasks delegated to them.

For managers, the reasons include:

- Trouble letting go of control
- Not wanting to devote time to work with an employee to explain the expectations

- Fear the employee will not do the job well and the manager will take the blame
- Worries they will be seen as lazy for not doing the job themselves
- Concern the employee will do the work better than they and they will be 'shown up' by them
- Having biases and preconceptions about certain employees and not trusting them

For employees/team members, the reasons include:

- Fear of being criticized for making mistakes
- Not having enough information to be able to perform the task
- Lack of self-confidence to be able to succeed
- Not having skills and expertise in the area
- Having a strained relationship with their superior [8]

If you recognize any of these as applicable to you, it is important to first spend time in reflection and introspection and second, to practice a direct and assertive approach to your team leader or member about what you need. That could be that you need more training, more time, more support from other team members, or simply that even with these, you do not feel you are the best choice for that task.

I can share a personal experience on this last scenario. I once had a CEO at a mid-sized company ask me to file a copyright with the federal government. I have zero legal training. I remember being so stunned I did not know how to respond. Finally, I asked why she chose me. She said because I was 'smart.' I told her this was not something I was comfortable doing, given the high stakes for the company and me professionally. She did find someone else at the company, equally unqualified, who took it on. Several months later, a cease-and-desist notice arrived because of a copyright violation. Lawyers had to be hired, the product could not be sold, and the company's reputation was tarnished.

Next, let's turn to one of the biggest challenges of professional communication—conflicts.

Managing Conflicts

We have a great deal of the self invested in our workplace. As people bring their personalities, needs, beliefs, values, expectations, and behaviors to work each day, it is almost a given that conflicts will arise and that these will be significant to us.

We can imagine how conflict in the workplace impacts the organization negatively, but it also has a negative impact on our well-being. If not addressed, we all face pressures and demands that will take their toll on our mental and physical well-being. This can manifest in such ways as anxiety, depression, high blood pressure, headache, inability to sleep, and strain on our other relationships outside of the workplace.[11]

Circling back to the organizational level, a study by Myers-Briggs found that the number one cause of workplace conflict cited by employees was poor communication. Further, 1 out of 4 believe their managers do not handle conflict well. Lastly, job satisfaction and feelings of belonging dropped the more someone dealt with workplace conflict.[12]

When conflict is unresolved, the workplace is dysfunctional.[13] People become emotionally detached; they put in less effort, they may call in sick frequently, and eventually will just leave. Resolving conflict, on the other hand, contributes to favorable work conditions, improved team dynamics, and individual growth.

Therefore, resolving conflicts more constructively is high on the priority list. We have covered in some detail how to resolve conflict with someone else. But now, let's look at some strategies for resolving conflict successfully in the workplace, particularly if it has escalated.

Choose A Facilitator

An objective facilitator can be helpful because of the likely high degree of emotion. It is important, however, to choose someone who has a track record of being able to do this task. Bringing another unskilled person into the mix will only make resolution more challenging. This means the immediate supervisor isn't always the de facto choice.

Establish Ground Rules

It can be helpful to have a set of basic guidelines. Without this, power and authority, as well as the type of communication style of an individual, can get in the way. The person with more power and authority may feel more enabled to interrupt, place blame, or just blow off the seriousness of the matter. People who are indirect or passive will be overshadowed. Rules such as remaining calm, not interrupting, refraining from blaming, and so on are good places to start.

Articulate The Issue

Each party needs the opportunity to share their perspective of the problem, why it occurred, what they have done to resolve it, and what they want to see happen. The facilitator can engage in and model active listening to get the facts as well as the perceptions out in the open.

Develop A Short List Of Solutions

These options must be constructed with input from the parties in conflict, not the facilitator. Otherwise, it's like a parent deciding how to resolve a conflict and then telling the kids to make up. The moment the parent leaves, the fighting starts again because they are not invested in a lasting solution.

Follow Up

The facilitator may now be out of the picture. The supervisor and other team members are the best ones to support the parties as they implement the solution. The conflict likely did not arise in one day (although a particular tipping point incident may have happened) and all the resentment, anger, and frustration aren't going to dissipate in one day either.

By working to resolve conflicts constructively with colleagues promptly and respectfully, the health of both the individuals and the organization is promoted.

One scenario where conflict is especially common is workplace feedback and so deserves additional attention. Let's take a closer look next.

Providing And Receiving Constructive Feedback

Feedback is a given element of the workplace. It can be formal or informal. It can be constructive or less than useful, even hurtful. In a majority of cases, managers and employees avoid it as much as they can.

Sherry Moss and Juan Sanchez are researchers in business leadership and cite a number of reasons for this. If we are on the receiving end of the feedback, there are psychological threats to our self-esteem, or we may have more concrete concerns such as worries about getting demoted, or even losing our job. [14]

Managers who see themselves as 'friendly' may be uncomfortable giving negative feedback. Those with unreasonable standards or a low tolerance for failure may expect they will get angry and not be able to keep their composure. Micro-managers can't parse out the important areas from the minutia.

When we receive harsh, destructive, or even random criticism about our performance, our natural inclination is to feel distress. This might be anger, frustration, hurt, anxiety or any combination. We can count on not being able to grow and develop—to improve.

If we are the one tasked with providing feedback, how can we do so in a way that will help the receiver to improve? Here are some strategies to use.

- Spend time before the feedback meeting or the writing of a report to try to understand the reasons for poor performance. Then, when meeting, guide the individual through the process to see which ones emerge. This will help you know how to focus your feedback.
- Use active listening techniques. Be fully present. Hold calls and ask that you all not be interrupted. Acknowledge your feelings as well as the receiver's that this might be a difficult conversation. An added tip is that if the feedback is negative, try to do this in private to avoid the receiver feeling humiliated and getting defensive.
- Resist the urge to rush through. If the feedback has the potential to be interpreted as negative, we may be tempted to check all the boxes and just get it over with. However, this superficial approach is counterproductive to the goal of helping the receiver improve.
- Stay focused on the concrete. Make it about task performance, not personality. As for suggestions for improving, give feedback that is specific, measurable, and achievable. Refer to any

documents or policies to keep it objective and supported.

- Involve the receiver. Ask what suggestions they have for improving, but don't put the entire burden on them. Additionally, you may have to shut down their blaming others. If they took a risk and failed, acknowledge this as a potential positive and talk through how to better execute in the future.

To help you better visualize what giving constructive feedback looks like, here are some examples.

"I like how enthusiastic you are during meetings. However, sometimes it's difficult for everyone to get a chance to share their ideas. Do you think you could hold off speaking until others have finished talking?"

"I appreciate your hard work on this project. I do notice a few gaps. For example, I didn't see last quarter's sales numbers. Can you share why that wasn't included?"

"I know working together with other departments can be challenging at times. How can we improve communication and collaboration with them?"

When you are on the receiving end, you can follow these same guidelines. Endeavor as well to get into a mindset that this is an opportunity for growth. Receive the feedback politely. If you feel it's not going well, here are some additional strategies to get back on track and gain value from the experience.

- Acknowledge the feedback. If there are points of misunderstanding, bring those out calmly.
- Ask for a written plan and set up a regular schedule to go over that plan.
- If you find your emotions getting the better of you, tell yourself you are strong enough to get through this and that you will take the time to process them later.
- If you have a poor communicator giving you feedback, try to guide them by keeping in mind the best practices listed above. In the meantime, seek feedback from someone you trust and respect.

To help you better visualize what receiving constructive feedback well looks like, here are some examples.

"That's a valid point. I appreciate you bringing that to my attention."

"You mention I'm not meeting goals. Can you give me a concrete example?"

"I'm looking to improve. Is there something specific I can do?"

"I'd like to think about what you've said and come up with a plan to work together with you. Would that be okay?"

When constructive feedback is a regular part of the workplace, it can be valuable tool for everyone's professional life!

Action Steps

We've covered quite a lot in this chapter, but let's recap some of the key action steps for you to take to improve workplace relationships and communication.

- Engage in active listening, with particular attention to how this technique can mitigate threats to accuracy, problem-solving, and efficiency in the workplace.
- Be firm but respectful when setting boundaries. Keep in mind the various situations, including physical, work-life balance, and mental/psychological.
- Hone your emotional intelligence skills. Be particularly alert to misunderstandings and their role in miscommunication.
- Engage with your team to create a shared vision, embrace the diverse perspectives of the members, and be sure to acknowledge and recognize the contributions of one another to promote collaboration.
- Work on giving and receiving feedback in an objective, concrete, and measurable way. Don't forget to make your professional development a priority in the process.

Chapter Summary

In this chapter, we explored how to create a healthy work environment by cultivating positive and mindful communication within professional settings, namely the workplace. Here are the key takeaways.

- Active listening is just as effective in building strong, positive relationships with a high degree of trust in the workplace as in other relationships.
- Establishing positive relationships is not only going to promote your well-being but will support the well-being of your organization. A part of this is establishing and maintaining appropriate boundaries.
- Collaborative teamwork is crucial in many workplace settings, and a key component is mastering the art of delegation.
- Conflicts are a natural part of the workplace as it comprises so many different perspectives and personalities. Because they can have significant negative impacts on the functioning of teams and the entire organization, often having an objective facilitator is more effective than handling a conflict on your own.
- Feedback is a natural part of the workplace, yet most of us want to avoid it. Using strategies to ensure it is constructive promotes the growth of the individuals and the entire organization.

A professional journey can last a very long time. By reflecting on and implementing the strategies covered in this chapter, you can continue to improve. You can ensure you are the consummate team player!

In the next chapter, we will take a close look at the common challenges in communicating with strangers and how to overcome these to have better relationships with people we do not yet know.

10

TURN STRANGERS INTO MEANINGFUL CONNECTIONS

HOW TO OVERCOME INITIAL HESITATIONS, BUILD YOUR CONFIDENCE, AND SPEAK WELL WITH PEOPLE OUTSIDE YOUR CIRCLE

My daughter had a part-time job at a bath and body store and was a favorite of the manager because she was able to upsell so well. Her secret? Making connections with strangers through the simple act of finding something on which to compliment them. This helped them warm up to her, which led to her recommending products they then purchased. Yet, after her shifts, she wasn't as excited about the sales as she was about the connections. Usually something like, "I met the nicest lady today!" "I had the best chat with a customer." It was clear these positive interactions with strangers enriched her life psychologically.

We've talked about the need for human connection, and have focused primarily on those people we already know, such as our family, friends, and co-workers. Yet, the benefits of social contact extend to interacting with people we don't yet know—strangers.

In this chapter, we will discuss the benefits of effective communication with strangers, the common barriers and challenges in communicating with people we don't know, and how to develop skills to overcome these obstacles.

Benefits Of Connecting With Strangers

Making connections with strangers may be short-lived, such as chatting on a plane or it may be the beginning of a long-lasting relationship. After all, if you think about it, all your friends and romantic partners were strangers to start!

Several research studies show that even fleeting interactions can give us the gift of well-being, such as a sense of belonging, happiness, learning, and creativity. Psychology researchers propose there are even benefits that interactions with strangers can give us that we can't get from our more intimate relationships—added value if you will.[1,2]

One is that it can be safer with regard to sensitive personal information. Because our family and friends are part of our larger social network, such information is more likely to be shared than by a stranger who isn't in our current network. Think, "Why are you so upset? I only told your Aunt Nancy!" You didn't want Aunt Nancy or anyone else to know, and it's even worse because you know she's the family gossip.

Two, we often gain a new perspective from strangers, and they may show more interest and curiosity in what we have to say than the people who already know us so well. Connecting with a stranger while you're both running the local marathon can be more enjoyable than talking to your elderly neighbor about your love of running.

Finally, you may stumble upon an opportunity which you might otherwise miss. It could be small, such as a recommendation for a great restaurant when visiting a new place, or more substantial, such as learning about a job position that's perfect for you.

Barriers To Connecting

Sadly, while we have more humans on the planet than at any other time, overall people are also lonelier. Some scholars call this a loneliness epidemic as we feel ever more isolated and disconnected from others.[3] Even though we see there is research, and more importantly, we likely have had positive encounters with strangers that 'made our day,' in general, studies show that most people are reluctant to approach strangers to interact.[2]

Why is this?

Stav Atir and colleagues are researchers in business and psychology and have proposed an evidence-based framework to help us better understand this phenomenon. The framework consists of three categories: intention, competence, and opportunity.[2] Let's take a closer look at each.

<u>Intention</u>

It turns out, we may not have a strong enough intention to talk to strangers because we underestimate the rewards and overestimate the burden.

For example, when researchers had people interact with strangers while commuting via public transportation, they felt happier afterward. People who only imagined how this kind of interaction would go believed it would be a negative experience.[4] Further, we tend to underestimate several other benefits, including how much we may learn, how much fun we will experience having the conversation, and how we might be judged.

Let's not forget that people also hold biases about those from backgrounds and cultures other than their own. This could be in the form of stereotypes or beliefs that we would not have enough in common to converse.

When it comes to interactions with strangers, some people fear they might be harmed. This could be due to a stereotype or bias, or it might be broader. For instance, a female may fear traveling alone or you may be fearful when a stranger knocks on your door late at night.

<u>Competence</u>

Another barrier to connecting with strangers is a lack of confidence in our ability to handle these interactions well. We are worried we won't know what to say or how to end the conversation smoothly. We are self-conscious that we won't be likable. We mistakenly think that asking questions may seem too pushy or that personal information is always oversharing. We don't realize that asking for guidance and advice doesn't mean that we are weak or incompetent.

Opportunity

The final area that represents a challenge is just having the opportunity to connect with others we don't know. This could be because we live in a sparsely populated area. Perhaps we are fully remote in our jobs and spend both our working and personal time at home. We may not have access to transportation. We may have a disability that makes it hard for us to go out in the community. Perhaps family obligations keep us more isolated, such as parenting small children or being the primary caretaker for an elderly or ill family member.

Social Anxiety

I want to spend a moment on social anxiety. While some people are more introverted, which makes them a bit more shy or reticent about social interactions, this is not the same as social anxiety. Social anxiety is a disorder with symptoms of fear and avoidance of social situations where someone feels they will be judged or evaluated.[5] This causes them to experience a great deal of distress which negatively impacts their ability to function. Meeting and interacting with strangers is a major trigger.

We have access to so much information, with certain conditions attracting a great deal of attention, and we may mistakenly misdiagnose ourselves. However, approximately 7% of adults in the U.S. do have social anxiety, and among those about a third fall into mild, moderate, and serious impairment respectively.[6] If you think you may have social anxiety that is impairing your ability to live fully, consider seeking guidance from a mental health professional.

Strategies To Overcome Stranger Connection Barriers

I hope that learning about the benefits, and knowing you are not alone if you find connecting with strangers challenging, motivates and excites you to tackle some strategies for furthering your social connections. We will break this up into smaller categories that follow the flow of an interaction.

Finding Opportunity

In order to engage with someone, you have to be in their presence. A stumbling block may be the belief that you have to put in a great deal of effort. If you feel you always have to find an event, a party, or a club and go all out on your appearance, for example, you are less likely to follow through.

While this kind of opportunity is certainly a good avenue for connecting with people you don't know, the random day-to-day encounters are important as well. They are perhaps better to start as they give you a low-stakes opportunity to hone your communication skills.

- Observe your surroundings to think of places where you can casually connect with strangers. Is it your bus stop, local coffee shop, or your child's playground? Perhaps your community is holding a festival or an art walk. If you live in a large city, consider joining a tourist group—you could meet people from all over the world.

- Consider where you can connect with like-minded people. Is there a place you can volunteer? Perhaps a soup kitchen, a pet shelter, or a nursing home. Many communities have classes. Then, there are as many clubs as there are interests. For classes and clubs, you can also connect virtually if these aren't available, or you aren't able to do something in person.

- Look at the places where there are the same people you may see very regularly but haven't had the confidence to make the first move to connect with. This could be your workplace, your religious organization, or your child's school. If you always eat your lunch at your cubicle, do so occasionally in the break room. If you dash in and dash out to pick up your child, consider going a few minutes early and hanging out with the other parents before release.

Improving Skills

By keeping the principles of mindful communication at the forefront and now that you are well-versed in the technique of active listening, these can help improve the conversations and connections you have with strangers.

Let's get a bit more specific with particular techniques to help you approach and then engage with people you don't know to connect and benefit your well-being.

'Read The Room.'

While many strangers will be open to interacting, even if briefly, some people are sending very strong signals that they are not, either as a matter of course or in the moment.

For instance, someone is deeply engrossed in a book, eating, wearing headphones, clearly in a hurry, dealing with a challenging situation, or their body language is very closed. Unless you are connecting to help a stranger in need, pass on trying to interact with that particular person.

When You Approach Someone, Do So At A Leisurely Relaxed Pace.

As you approach, once in place, be respectful of personal space. Otherwise, you may come across as intimidating or threatening.

Body Language And Other Forms Of Nonverbal Communication Play An Enormous Role In Communication With Strangers.

Smile warmly and genuinely. Make eye contact, but only hold someone's gaze a few seconds. Longer will make most people uncomfortable. Take a relaxed stance. Tilt your body toward the person or if appropriate, face the person.

Begin The Conversation Simply And With Some Component That Generates A Response.

A simple "Hello, how's it going?" "This is my first time on this train. Is it usually on time?" "I'm just getting into wine. Do you have any recommendations?" "I love your scarf. Can I ask what material it is?" If you are in a situation where there is shared interest, you have an automatic topic of conversation!

By keeping it simple, and yes, somewhat superficial, the person doesn't have to immediately start wondering what you want. Remember the cost part of the equation? It's natural to be a little suspicious.

Go Deeper Once You Have Established Someone Wants To Engage With You.

You can ask them questions about themselves. As people, most of us like talking about ourselves. This also takes the pressure off you to be interesting because your energy is on being interested in them.

Start with non threatening topics to put them at ease. Try questions like, "What do you like to do in your spare time?" "How long have you been….?" "How do you like living here?" Then, if it is more than a brief interaction, or if you see them again, you can move to more meaningful topics, such as "I'm struggling with balancing work with my personal life. Does that ever happen to you?" "I just became a first-time dad. I feel like I'm boring everyone talking about my son all the time. I know you have two kids, is this normal?"

Avoid Being Overly Negative And Disgruntled.

If you come across as too whiny, it can be off-putting. However, there are some areas where you may commiserate, like lousy weather or long lines, but, in general, try to remain in positive territory.

Stay Away From Highly Charged Topics Because You May Inadvertently Put Someone Off.

That said, if you do plan to make a stranger into a friend, there may be places where you hold such fundamental differences that while you can respectfully be acquaintances, this person may not become a part of your inner social circle.

Bonus tip: *Pace your conversation by taking some deep breaths and waiting a second or two to give the other person time and space to respond.*

While you may assume the approach and interaction are the most important components of connecting with a stranger, the way you close the interaction can make a substantial difference to whether the social connection is viable. Not only on the impression you leave but how you feel later as you reflect on the experience.

You've had a nice exchange, but it's time to move on. This is fairly easy if the environment is set up for this, "Well, this is my stop. It was nice to chat!" but sometimes it is more awkward. This is one of the purposes behind speed dating. Figuring out how to end and move on is taken out of the hands of the participants!

If you are at an event or function, you will likely need to politely break away, perhaps because you want to speak to others. It could be that the conversation you are having is losing momentum. You could be running out of mental steam and need a break.

Here are some examples for you to consider. "I just realized I didn't say "Hello" to our host yet, so I'd better do that now. It was great meeting you!" "Have fun on your tour!" "I'm seeing the time! I have a super early meeting. It was a pleasure talking with you!" "I'll let you get back to your shopping, but I really enjoyed hearing about the recipe you're going to make."

One thing to keep in mind is that while we have been talking about how you can better interpret cues, other people may not be skilled in this area. You can use additional body language and nonverbal signals. Put a little distance between you and the person. Turn your body away a bit. Gaze away now and again. Just nod, but don't verbally participate.

If you think you'd like to interact with this person again, and circumstances permit, go ahead and put that out there. You will likely be able to tell quite quickly if the feeling is mutual. "This was great. Maybe we can have lunch sometime?" "I know both our husbands play basketball on Saturdays. It would be great to chat some more." "It was fun to talk to you. I'll send you a Facebook friend request if that's okay."

By using strategies such as these, you can create a road map to higher quality interactions with strangers. Like any skill, it takes practice. While you might be self-conscious at first, with time, you will reap the benefits of bringing more meaningful connections with others into your life.

Figure 10.1 Getting to know new people can be initimidating but brings rewarding connections.[7]

Building Connections Through Networking

We've concentrated on connections that occur more casually and spontaneously, but let's now look at a more structured and planned avenue for making connections—networking.

Networking is a process where we actively seek to meet others who share our goals and interests to make connections and build relationships. This can be to enhance our professional or personal lives. If you look at a typical conference program, there will almost always be dedicated time for networking. In areas that might be based on more personal interests, these are often called 'meet and greets.' Some events are exclusively for this purpose.

Networking offers a plethora of benefits, from building confidence to sharing knowledge to advancing our careers. For example, research shows that many career outcomes are positively associated with networking, including successful job searching, promotions, salary level, performance on the job, and career satisfaction.[8]

Networking usually has the end goal of a more lasting relationship, or at least one where we get more from the experience than a pleasant chat, although that's part of it hopefully. In networking, we want to purposively expand our social circle. We want to capture opportunities.

When we engage in networking we have an advantage. We know that if we go to an event or reach out on a social networking site, the people there are more likely to be open to connecting because they are there for the same reason. The popularity of social networking sites like Facebook and LinkedIn expands our networking opportunities even further, as we can connect with people we otherwise might never be able to outside of our physical location.

That said, online networking is often more effective as a channel for communication to reinforce a budding relationship than to make new ones. While we can have many connections, if these are just for show, the benefits will likely not be realized.

People who extend their authentic social networking connections to the online sphere have more emotional closeness in these relationships. If managed well, most people experience a sense of happiness and excitement. However, there is also the potential for people to experience negative outcomes, such as a knock to their self-esteem or becoming apprehensive about communicating if they receive undesirable feedback.[9]

To help you make the most of your social networking opportunities, let's look next at some strategies you can try.

Strategies For Effective Networking

We've talked about strategies to approach strangers, and you will want to bring those with you to your networking game. However, several other strategies are unique to networking. Let's dive into those now.

Setting Goals

Setting realistic and achievable goals before launching into networking can help you stay focused and keep your motivation high. This isn't to say that you can't have fun and enjoy yourself, but rather that you prepare a bit so that you can make the most of the opportunity. On the other hand, taking it too seriously and having expectations set too high can lead to disappointment.

You might think of your goals as immediate, short-term, medium-term, and long-term. For career-oriented networking, an immediate goal could be to have a conversation with three people. A short-term goal would be to set up a follow-up meeting with at least two of them. A medium-term goal could be a joint project with one of them. A long-term goal would be to sit on their advisory board.

For a personal networking situation, an immediate goal could be to meet the president of the PTA (Parent-Teacher Association). A short-term goal would be to become a PTA volunteer. A medium-term goal could be to have a lower level position on the PTA board. A long-term goal would be to become the PTA president when that position is available.

Doing Your Homework

Research the people who will be at the networking event or who are in your current network. Check out their social media, read anything they may have written, and look for their bios. This will not only help you narrow down your time and resources, but when you do have that chance to speak to them you will be seen more favorably if you know a bit about them.

First Impressions

I mentioned in the first part of the chapter that often some people are so worried about how they will be perceived that they are almost paralyzed to get out and interact with people they don't know. I encouraged you not to get too caught up in this. However, if you are attending a networking event, or considering creating your online profile, you do need to be attentive to the small details.

Most of us are restricted in the number of networking events we can attend or the time we can spend on social networking sites, so putting in the effort at the top can reap benefits later. This is different than having a casual conversation at the local community theater while waiting in line to see a play. Remember, networking is more focused, more purposeful.

In person, you want to dress appropriately for starters. If you aren't sure what to wear, go one step up but not all the way to your most formal. Pay attention to your body language, tone, and voice volume, and aim for the middle. You don't want to be too exuberant, nor do you want to come across as stiff and awkward. Make sure this translates to your handshake.

When creating your online profile, try to choose your name rather than a nickname or something clever. Choose a flattering picture that fits the site—casual for personal, more formal for professional.

I can't resist sharing an amusing personal anecdote here. I had a very close friend who became a widow. After several years of not meeting anyone, she decided to join an online dating site. She wasn't particularly tech-savvy so she asked her daughter to help her. I was visiting and she happened to mention that she was disappointed that she had not received more interest. I was surprised because she was very attractive and, of course, on sites like these that is often the deciding factor for a first connection.

She asked if I would take a look at her profile and give her my thoughts. The first thing I noticed was that the profile picture was one of her in a giant red parka. You could barely see her face at all. I commented on this and she said that was the photo her daughter selected so she went with it. I couldn't help but put two and two together that her daughter was struggling with her mother moving on and dating and had, subconsciously perhaps, sabotaged the process with likely the most unflattering photo she could find. When I pointed this out, we both couldn't help but laugh.

- *Networking Etiquette*

Etiquette is important in society because it represents a common code for our behavior in a group. Etiquette helps everyone know what to do—it supports interactions, moving comfortably along politely and respectfully. Calling on what you have learned about emotional intelligence can help you here.

When networking, whether in person or online, etiquette means you will want to aim for confidence but not pushiness. Approach people as though you belong and that you will be well received. Avoid being too eager but be alert and attentive.

Practice the art of small talk to break the ice and build rapport. Create a short list of topics that match the situation if you can. In personal networking, this might be pets, food, or travel. In professional networking, ask about their career choice or a project they've just completed. Bringing up people who are mutual connections can make an instant good impression.

Do remember to listen more than you speak. You want to learn as much as you can about the other person to determine if this would be a good connection for you.

- *Following Up.*

This is key. As we mentioned, you do not want just to begin a relationship, you want to maintain and expand the connection. As soon as you can, depending on the situation and the person, send a text, email, a friend request, or a connection request and message on LinkedIn. When the interaction is over, be sure to graciously thank the person for their time, let them know you enjoyed meeting them, and that you are looking forward to continuing the conversation.

Figure 10.2 A typical networking event[10]

By utilizing these strategies, you can be well on your way to a successful networking experience and making those meaningful social connections with people you don't know.

I'd like to close with a challenge that allows you to test the power of your social networks, especially if you don't typically harness it. Set a realistic goal to get your network to take action on something you initiate. I don't mean, "If you are truly my friend, you will like this post," which I see often. I mean something authentic and meaningful. Here are some examples of what this might look like.

- You volunteer at the local pet shelter. Can you get one dog or cat adopted this month?

- You write a blog for your company. Can you get 20 people to share it?
- You are planning a neighborhood garage sale. Can you get five families to participate?
- You are looking for a new position. Can you get two leads?

Once you start doing this on a small scale and see success, remembering to be persistent, you will have the confidence to go bigger and better. Let me share an example.

My colleague and I were tasked with conducting 100 interviews with neurologists, neuroradiologists, and neurosurgeons and we had just six weeks to do this. These people are incredibly busy and fiercely protective of their time, understandably so. My colleague is a neuroscientist, and it was only due to his dedicated effort to building and actively maintaining his social network that we were able to pull this off successfully.

Action Steps

We've covered many strategies, but here are some overall action steps for you to take to improve your social interaction skills with people you do not yet know.

- Reflect on the benefits you will gain by connecting with strangers, keeping in mind that these can be powerful for your well-being.

- Think about the barriers and which ones are most likely to be stumbling blocks for you. Develop a strategy to tackle these.
- While there are many nuances, concentrate on becoming more emotionally intelligent and practicing active listening to build a solid foundation for social connections with strangers.
- Engage in a mix of casual spontaneous encounters and more planned goal-oriented networking.

Chapter Summary

As we close this chapter, we have learned about making connections with strangers. Here are some key takeaways for you.

- Whether fleeting or long-lasting, connections with strangers improve our well-being. We also reap benefits we may not always get from our more intimate relationships, such as a feeling of safety when sharing personal information or finding that we have shared interests.
- Most people are reluctant when it comes to approaching strangers. This is because we think it will be a hardship or negative when the research shows the opposite. We also build up in our minds that we will be incompetent—not good at it.

- We can improve our social connection skills by finding opportunities; paying attention to social cues, and practicing starting, maintaining, and ending conversations confidently.
- Networking is a powerful tool we have at our disposal. By setting goals, knowing our potential connections, using etiquette, and following up, we can increase our social circle and grow personally and professionally.

Connecting with strangers can be intimidating. You may feel uneasy for some time, but once you have a few positive interactions, you will find that your day is brighter, your life is fuller, and you are more fulfilled for having taken that step to talk to a stranger. I hope that you, too, can regularly say, "I had the best chat today!"

It's hard to believe, but we are coming near the end. We have one more vitally important topic to cover in Chapter 11. We will explore how mindful communication can drive social change and raise awareness for important causes.

11

THE TALK THAT CHANGES THE WORLD

HOW TO USE YOUR VOICE TO UPLIFT OTHERS
AND BE A FORCE OF POSITIVE CHANGE

O ne of the most iconic awareness and advocacy campaigns in the United States was from 'Keep America Beautiful.' Run on network television, it featured a man dressed as a Native American canoeing in a modern river full of trash and landing on an equally polluted riverbank. At just one minute in length, there was dramatic music, some overlay audio, and the final scene of a single tear rolling down the man's cheek. The announcer ends with a statement that some people have respect for natural beauty, while others do not.

This ad aired in the 1970s and was widely seen and discussed. It made a definite impression. The origin turned out to be troubling, however. Not widely known until later, the campaign was at the behest of a big corporation, primarily packaging and drink companies, which comprised a large portion of the Keep America Beautiful board.[1] These corporations did not want to be held responsible for the then novel invention of single-use bottles.

The solution? Communicate that the individual is personally responsible for litter.

Yet, even in the midst of knowing this now, I can attest from personal experience that the ad did make a difference on an individual level. We thought more carefully. We picked up other people's trash. Fast forward, and we have recycling. Communities are banning single-use plastic. Upcycling is now trendy.

This example highlights that advocacy for social change is not a simple task. It rarely moves in a straight line. Communication is at the heart, whether in words or images, and it too is not simple in this context. In this final chapter, we concentrate on the vital role of mindful communication in advocacy—how it can raise awareness for positive social change and why such communication and conversation are transformative.

We will also look at the inevitable obstacles, many of which are related to ourselves as well as the nature of the online and digital environment. We will discuss strategies to use mindful communication to drive social change and raise awareness for causes that are significant to us.

Social Change Through Communication

Whether standing on a box in the town square, handing out pamphlets to passersby, or posting online in forums, people have been using communication to affect social change for centuries until the present day. In many instances, this is as a collective. A group of people are organized and have a specific goal in mind. Their efforts are typically directed toward a particular group, usually one seen as having authority. This is frequently the government or big corporations.

Many forms of communication are employed. In addition to those already mentioned, these could be forming an association with a mission and bylaws, making statements to the press, or marching with signs. Charles Tilly was a well-known 20th-century sociologist, political scientist, and historian. He posited that social movements have, and will continue to be, in response to socio-political events. The specific social cause may change, but the mechanism and process will remain largely the same.[2]

Emile McAnany has worked for five decades in the field of social and cultural communication for development (scholars use the term 'development' to indicate such communication is related to growth and positive movement). In his book *Saving the World: A Brief History of Communication for Development and Social Change*," McAnany notes that while the field of communications recognizes our global interconnectedness in the modern world, institutions that are on the front lines of giving aid do not seem to give communication as much attention.[3]

McAnany issues a call to action that communication needs a central role in social change. I find it interesting that he makes a point to highlight that it is not policies, programs, or funding alone that historically have made a difference in improving people's lives, but rather people's participation in such opportunities. Given McAnany's expert perspective, I think this is an important point for us all to consider.

To set the stage for this chapter, let's look at a couple of examples of how communication has made a significant contribution to positive social change.

The #MeToo Movement illustrates how effective communication enabled victims of sexual harassment and assault to be empowered to share their stories worldwide. This made it more acceptable to discuss topics that had been considered taboo. This is leading to a cultural shift and changes in policies in the workplace, on college campuses, and the like.[4]

The United Nations has a global initiative for universal access to clean water. It uses communication to raise awareness, as well as to mobilize resources, and track the progress being made. They have recently agreed on stronger guidelines for their strategic communications, such as through websites using the local language both at the organization *and* community levels.[5]

Misinformation And Disinformation

Before we go further, it is useful to introduce and define two specific threats to communication around social change. These threats are present in our discussions with one another and frequently have their origins in where we get much of our information—the media. They are especially prevalent in digital media, most notably on social media platforms, which we will discuss more fully later in the chapter.

Misinformation is fake or misleading information that is spread or shared unintentionally, meaning it is not known to be untrue by those who do so. Conversely, disinformation is also fake and misleading, but it is spread and shared intentionally, meaning those who do so are aware it is untrue.[6]

<u>Raising Awareness</u>

To take action, one must first be aware of an issue, along with the pros and cons of any solution, whether that be an innovation, an initiative, a product, a service, or some activity.[7] Only then can motivation emerge for change.

Communication about highly charged social issues must be accurate. For example, as citizens of Western countries, we may think that taking our fast-fashion clothing to a thrift store means doing something positive. However, we may not be as aware that such facilities cannot manage the volume. In many instances, our clothing waste is sold and shipped overseas to primarily low-income countries, where it fills their landfills and now overflows into their waterways, greenways, and even parks.[7]

Going back to the United Nations and its clean water initiative, public health researchers Sohaib Mustafa and colleagues looked closely at public awareness to help achieve this goal. Billions of individuals around the world still do not have access to clean drinking water or basic sanitation. Many such countries have a high poverty level. These citizens may not be on board for the government to fund initiatives for clean water nor are they open to paying for it directly because the citizens are not aware of the importance of clean water to their health. Because public awareness is so strongly related to positive behavioral change, the United Nations has for many years been directing a great deal of its communication resources to public awareness campaigns.[8]

Not being fully aware and informed means we cannot take the next step—to be good advocates.

Inspiring Advocacy

Whereas awareness is at the individual level, advocacy efforts are more at the group level. The underlying definition of advocacy is quite simple. Advocacy is when there is public support for a cause. That cause may benefit us directly, indirectly, or not at all and rather on behalf of others. That cause can be just an idea all the way to a fully developed plan of action.

What all advocacy movements have in common is the use of public communication in service of the cause.[9] Such communication is strategic—meaning it is carefully designed, deliberate, and targeted. The goal is that policies or initiatives result that can promote social change.

Let's also take a moment to look at the difference between an advocate and an activist. Both are committed to seeing positive change, but an advocate does so more for a specific individual or group, while an activist desires change at a much broader level. As an advocate for the environment, I might become a member of the Sierra Club and donate or volunteer for a beach cleanup. As an activist for the environment, however, I might start or join a public protest against any of the major oil companies that have spilled oil in the ocean.

There are many examples of advocacy efforts resulting in positive social change. For example, civil rights, public schooling, fair wages, or the ALS Ice Bucket Challenge.

Let's take a look at how communication enabled over one million dollars to be raised for ALS (amyotrophic lateral sclerosis) research in a short period. You may remember it was by video. Videos that went viral and got people sharing the message and talking about the cause, which previously had been mostly unknown to the general public. The idea was simple yet extremely effective. People shared videos pouring ice-cold water over their heads, and nominated others to participate, all while donating.

A remarkable 17 million people have done the Ice Bucket Challenge to date. As a result, the ALS Association has been able to greatly expand their annual research funding by 187% and doubled their care within local communities.[10] This campaign also did more than bring this devastating disease to the forefront. It brought to our attention the actual people, and their loved ones, who suffer. It elicited our empathy for our fellow men and women.

Figure 11.1 Woman splashed with cold water similar to the Ice Bucket Challenge.[11]

Mindful Communication And Social Causes

Sydnee Viray and Robert Nash are social justice educators. They state that "advocacy calls for empathy, patience, determination, nonjudgmentalism, and humility" (p. 20)[12] Of course, these traits are also at the heart of mindful communication. And this is at the core of Viray and Nash's case when discussing what they consider the most challenging obstacle to successful advocacy outcomes—what they call "madvocacy." This is using anger, being indignant or outraged, spreading rumors, and/or laying on the guilt in an attempt to change someone's thinking. The result? Enemies rather than allies.

It is important, however, to point out that some degree of anger or alarm is necessary to rally efforts for social change. One of the most insidious roadblocks is complacency. Think, "It's not my problem," "You can't fight the man," or "I'm sure this will pass in time." The point is that always being a "madvocate," as Viray and Nash termed it, will just alienate those you are trying to convince who may be complacent. For those who are not complacent but have an opposing view, such an approach will only further divide you both as you each become further entrenched in your own camp.

That said, the good news is that all you have learned about mindful communication can serve you well in your efforts to affect positive social change. Bring your compassion and empathy to the table when you have conversations. Use what you know about active listening and nonviolent communication to help you foster that meaningful connection with someone else. This will prompt deeper and more solution-oriented dialogue. Everyone will be more inspired!

Further, when we work together in the service of advocacy, we can lean on one another for support and motivation. It can be daunting and discouraging to tackle difficult issues. Having honest and vulnerable conversations about our feelings, or listening with compassion to others, makes not just the individual, but the entire group stronger.

Next, we turn to the place where conversations around social injustices abound and advocacy efforts can pick up enormous momentum, yet where one must tread with care and skill to keep true to mindful communication— the digital world.

Communication In A Digital Landscape

Technology has always played a pivotal role in changes to our communication. We use smartphones to make calls no matter where we are, rather than from a public phone booth or a landline in our home or office. We no longer rely just on writing letters but instead text our friends. Print newspapers and magazines are virtually nonexistent because we get our information on the internet. We convey to companies worldwide who we are as professionals on LinkedIn rather than sending resumes to a select few. When we see something we agree or disagree with, we post a comment immediately rather than writing a letter to the editor. Today's technology means we can instantly communicate with millions of other people or a single person.

The way we express ourselves with regard to the specific interactions in a digital manner frequently differs from in person. Our writing is more informal, as we may not even use complete sentences, capitalization, or punctuation. We make greater use of images, such as photos, memes, or emojis. We may even express ourselves without a specific individual in mind when we write blogs or post videos online.

Communicating digitally has downsides and benefits.[13] This method can be more impersonal. Instead of having conversations in our neighborhood or community, we have them online. We can also put our priority into online communication and neglect it within our own circle of family and friends. We have all likely seen, or perhaps personally experienced, being out to dinner with the family, and everyone is looking at their phone rather than conversing. Over time, this can increase feelings of loneliness.

We also miss out on the richness that can come with in-person communication. We aren't able to experience the nonverbal or observe social cues as accurately. We may not even know someone's name—just their social media handle. We may not use our best manners when we have the cloak of anonymity.

But there are distinct benefits. These include speed and consistency. We are able to connect with people we would never be able to do so with otherwise. It also makes it much easier to maintain relationships and stay in touch with those in our close circle. Finally, we can gather our thoughts before sending that email, text, or comment. All these support social connectivity.

The capabilities of digital communication also means it is more possible than ever to find others who share our interests and concerns. As mentioned before in this book, being a part of a group is essential for our well-being as people. One particular mechanism for group membership is very instrumental—social media. We turn there next, with particular attention to the association between social media and social causes.

The Power Of Social Media For Social Change

Let's begin with defining social media. This is a collective term that relates to communicating ideas and information among a large number of people. This can take many forms. It could be a blog, image/video site, or a social networking site. Most of us are quite active users of social media. According to the Pew Research Center, as of 2023, the most popular platforms for U.S. adults are YouTube and Facebook, and almost half report using Instagram.[14]

Sociologists Dustin Kidd and Keith McIntosh write extensively about social media and social movements. They have an interesting take and lay out three types of views. One is "techno-optimism." This is where the potential of social media to affect social change is emphasized, although some obstacles are acknowledged. There is also "techno-pessimism" where the potential of social media is thought to be over-inflated, surface-level, ripe with mis/disinformation, and therefore unable to make any meaningful change.

Lastly, is "techno-ambivalence." Here, there is uncertainty or ambiguity because harnessing social media isn't going to be successful automatically, nor is it a foregone conclusion that it will fail—it could go either way. Kidd and McIntosh support this view because it means there is a possibility, but we aren't naïve enough to think that social change via social media can occur without care and effort.[15]

Let's look at some examples of when social media campaigns tip to the side of getting it right. The Centers for Disease Control did a campaign called "Tips from Former Smokers," and as a result, 1 million people quit smoking, almost 130,000 early deaths were prevented, and their hotline has had a dramatic surge of callers.[16]

Ocean Bottle has 1 billion TikTok users every month. Their #econfession campaign encouraged people to share when they slipped up being eco-friendly. For every post, it stopped 10 plastic bottles from going into the ocean through paying local collectors in countries without good waste disposal.[17]

Practicing Mindful Communication In Social Causes When Online

While these examples are positive, as we have briefly mentioned, there are pitfalls when engaging in advocacy when online. Let's look at some of these as you think about engaging to impact positive social change in the fast-moving digital environment.

Figure 11. 2 Everyone has access to digital platforms nowadays.[18]

Communications researchers Michael Kent and Maureen Taylor note that the momentum of a particular effort can be deceiving because popularity in online platforms is measured in counts such as likes and shares. However, this does not measure meaningful engagement and dialogue.[19] Certain platforms are not designed for deep discussions of the complexities of certain issues like inequality, climate change, or immigration. Additionally, users' skills vary widely with regard to engaging in respectful and informed discussion. People may be uncomfortable at the prospect of being criticized or attacked or they may use these methods primarily themselves and alienate others.

That said, Kent and Taylor offer an approach to have more meaningful and evolved conversations through the lens of "dialogic engagement." This includes:

- Valuing others
- Respect
- Taking turns
- Having numerous interactions
- Collaborating
- Mutually satisfying activities
- Allowing others to reach their own conclusions. [19]

As you may see, dialogic engagement is very similar and much aligned with mindful communication. With this framework in place, let's turn now to strategies relating to advocacy.

Strategies For Mindful Online Communication & Advocacy

With all this as a backdrop, here are some specific strategies to use mindful communication when engaging online for advocacy for positive social change.

Active Listening. Engage fully and be present. Avoid interrupting others or denigrating their point of view. Using "I" statements keeps the feeling of blame down. Being open to other perspectives means that both you and the person you are engaging with may learn something important. Rather than "How dare you say that to me!" try, "I didn't fully understand your point. Can you tell me a bit more about why you believe I am wrong on this issue?"

<u>Manage Your Emotions</u>. When people are advocating for a cause that is meaningful to them, they can get quite passionate. Interacting with someone who is in opposition to that cause can result in heightened emotions on both sides.

When you feel you are being criticized, think about the importance of managing your emotions. Doing so will allow you to see this conflict as an opportunity for growth. It is key to consider your tone and the language you use. Rather than personally attacking or calling someone an unkind name, focus instead on the issue. For example, once you call someone stupid for example, it's probably game over. Also, remember our discussion of "madvocates?" This translates to "keyboard warrior" when online. Pausing before responding can help you avoid impulsively reacting when your emotions are running high.

<u>Get The Facts Straight</u>. Misinformation and disinformation are, unfortunately, rampant. Not only is this critical for being an effective advocate, it is important for being ethical. Rather than just take what you see online as the truth, do invest some time in researching from reputable sources. You neither want to be a victim of misinformation/disinformation or unwittingly spread misinformation. Here are some tips.

- The author is listed and has a bio you can read. This allows you to determine if they are qualified to write/speak on the topic.

- The information is based on evidence, cited, and current. The message seems complete and not "cherry-picked" to only highlight part of the full story or only one perspective. We want the full story as well as to try to avoid confirmation bias, where we only interact with others who see the issues the way we do.
- In general, the website is an education, research, or government site as opposed to a company that may have an agenda to sell something. You can also look to see who is funding the source.

Pick Your Battles. There are thousands of issues that need attention, but it is impossible to be an advocate for all of them. I would recommend that rather than using your head, you use your heart. What resonates with you? What matters to you? Where do you feel you could contribute and maintain involvement?

In advocacy, quality over quantity often results in change. Focused, concentrated effort is needed. When you do advocacy well, you also serve as a role model for others, even if their issue of interest is different.

This also ties into maintaining healthy boundaries. This can mean taking a break from screens and the relentless information this brings into our lives. It lessens burnout and gives you a chance to do something in the real world that brings a sense of calm and peace. In this way, you can recharge and stay balanced.

Let's look at a scenario where this comes together.

Jamal is passionate about environmental issues. He's aware that he can use social media to advocate for sustainable practices in his community but knows that people have strong opinions in this area, so he wants to take a mindful approach. He first takes some time to decide the specific issues where he feels he can make a meaningful impact.

Jamal then spends time following environmental groups and experts to understand different perspectives and concerns. Along the way, he engages with their content to show support and learn more about the evidence and latest developments in the field.

As he suspected, there is controversy, and he finds himself having to be keep from reacting impulsively. When he feels like he's getting worked up, he takes a deep breath and pauses so that he can respond calmly and respectfully, even when he is on the receiving end of criticism. He also makes sure to verify sources and double-check data to ensure his posts are accurate. Jamal finds this helps him avoid getting drawn into unproductive debates.

After a while, these strategies begin to pay off, and Jamal finds that he is inspiring others to join him in creating positive change for the environment.

Action Steps

We've discussed quite a lot as we reflect on awareness and advocacy for social change. Here are some overall action steps for you to put into practice.

- Keep reminding yourself that you can make a meaningful contribution to advocacy efforts to see positive social change but not everyone has to be an activist.
- Think about what matters most to you and concentrate your efforts there.
- Use all the mindful communication skills you have gained throughout this book in this arena, being especially aware of misinformation and disinformation and avoiding becoming a "madvocate" and "keyboard warrior."

Chapter Summary

As we come to the end of this chapter, I hope you have gained insight and confidence about how you can have meaningful, respectful conversations with others as you engage in the issues of importance to you. It can be daunting to participate and difficult to maneuver the nuances. Here are some key takeaways to keep in mind.

- Communication for social change can take many forms, but at the core, it's about people participating over just the specific policies, initiatives, and programs.
- Awareness is the first step and is usually at the individual level, followed by concerted advocacy efforts, which is when the power of the group emerges. It's especially crucial to be on the lookout for misinformation and disinformation.

- Effective advocacy has empathy at its core. When we have conversations about difficult and highly charged issues, keeping this central will allow us to truly connect to solve big problems.
- Communicating well digitally takes thought and effort, but we have the priceless benefit of being able to connect with many others for advocacy momentum...and motivation.

Congratulations—you have made it through all the chapters. In the next section, we will bring all we have learned together in the Conclusion.

AFTERWORD

I once worked with the CEO of a startup who was having trouble with her executive team. She felt the project was not moving forward quickly enough. A lot was riding on getting a product launched and, understandably, tensions were high in the whole team. As we got started, she wanted the team members to first share their viewpoints on the project pace before she did.

However, you could see her getting more and more agitated. As the last person began to speak, she interrupted and said quite loudly, "I don't want to hear what you all think we should do. I just want you to do what I say!" You could practically feel the shockwaves from her team. This one statement showed just how out of alignment the team was.

Where did the fault lie? Before reading this book, you might have said it was squarely with the CEO. But now, you likely know that everyone was contributing to the poor communication. The team were experts and seasoned executives. They felt it was their job to participate at a very deep level and to make sure everything was perfect before launch. Of course, in theory, the CEO valued this, or she would not have hired them. But she was under the most pressure, both financially and reputationally.

No one was reading the cues, being clear about their needs, or putting themselves in the shoes of the others. To progress and make sure the project was successful, we had to stop talking about the work and start tackling the communication issues. Fortunately, by applying many of the learnings and techniques in this book, over time the team was able to work together more effectively and the product launched close to the deadline.

Let's recap the key takeaways from *5 Rules To Improve Your Conversations: How to find your voice, communicate with empathy to resolve conflicts and improve relationships at work, home, or anywhere.*

Our five rules are:

1. Practice mindful communication.
2. Use the power of self-awareness.
3. Listen. Do not just hear.
4. Practice empathy and cultural intelligence.
5. Do not be afraid to face conflicts as part of communicating.

As humans, we need secure intimate relationships for our emotional well-being. Rather than ineffective conversations marked by misunderstanding and, ultimately, alienation, mindful communication allows compassionate and empathetic conversations where healthy and deep relationships flourish.

Self-communication is an essential part of the equation for improving conversations and relationships. Through inner dialogue with self-reflection and introspection, you can experience meaningful personal growth. Being self-aware and acknowledging our biases ensures our needs are met and also that others are treated well, no matter their culture or background.

Built on empathy and emotional support, active listening is a powerful communication technique. When life's inevitable conflicts arise, dialogue is a vital mechanism for finding a "win-win" solution. Every relationship has unique dynamics, but aiming for direct and assertive communication rather than indirect or passive-aggressiveness fosters stronger connections.

Creating a healthy work environment is possible by setting appropriate boundaries, collaborating, and solving conflict rather than letting it fester. Connecting with strangers by finding and seizing opportunities and practicing our conversation skills with confidence improves our personal and professional lives. Having conversations about difficult and highly-charged issues with empathy will allow us to connect to solve big problems.

Communication involves understanding yourself, the other person, and the specific dynamics and various settings where we have interactions. Moving past what we might have previously thought about conversations as just casual "chitchat," your conversations can be meaningful dialogue that help you find your voice, communicate with empathy to resolve conflicts, and improve relationships.

My hope is that you will continue to reflect on the research and key takeaways, practice the strategies, and share what you have learned with others. Thank you for allowing me to be your guide on this journey. I wish you many opportunities to say, "I just had the greatest conversation!"

REFERENCES

Introduction

1. Young, K. S., Parsons, C. E., Jegindoe Elmholdt, E. M., Woolrich, M. W., Van Hartevelt, T. J., Stevner, A. B., ... & Kringelbach, M. L. (2016). Evidence for a caregiving instinct: Rapid differentiation of infant from adult vocalizations using magnetoencephalography. Cerebral Cortex, 26(3), 1309-1321. https://doi.org/10.1093/cercor/bhv306

1. Do Your Words Matter?

1. silviarita. (2019). *Girl, Woman, Pressure to perform* [Photograph]. Pixabay. https://pixabay.com/photos/girl-woman-pressure-to-perform-4118072/
2. Baer, R. A., Smith, G. T., Hopkins, J., Krietemeyer, J., & Toney, L. (2006). Using self-report assessment methods to explore facets of mindfulness. *Assessment, 13*(1), 27-45. https://doi.org/10.1177/1073191105283504
3. Littlejohn, S. W., & Foss, K. A. (2010). *Theories of human communication.* Waveland Press.
4. Adler, R. B., & Rodman, G. (2019). *Understanding human connection.* Oxford University Press.
5. Burgoon, J. K., Berger, C. R., & Waldron, V. R. (2000). Mindfulness and interpersonal communication. *Journal of Social Issues, 56*(1), 105-127.
6. No_Name13. (2016). *Tic tac toe, Heart, Game* [Photograph]. Pixabay. https://pixabay.com/photos/tic-tac-toe-heart-game-chalk-love-1777859/
7. osenberg, M. B., & Chopra, D. (2015). *Nonviolent communication: A language of life: Life-changing tools for healthy relationships.* PuddleDancer Press.
8. Sung, J., & Kweon, Y. (2022). Effects of a nonviolent communication-based empathy education program for nursing students. *Nursing Reports, 12*(4), 824-835. https://doi.org/10.3390/nursrep12040080

9. Duchscherer, D. (2004). *Nonviolent communication as core principle for any public policy to prevent humiliation dynamics*. In Short Note Prepared for the" Workshop on Humiliation and Violent Conflict," November (pp. 18-19).

10. Koopman, S., & Seliga, L. (2021). Teaching peace by using nonviolent communication for difficult conversations in the college classroom. *Peace and Conflict Studies*, *27*(3), 2. https://doi.org/10.46743/1082-7307/2021.1692

11. Frei, J. R., & Shaver, P. R. (2002). Respect in close relationships: Prototype definition, self-report assessment, and initial correlates. *Personal Relationships*, *9*(2), 121-139. https://doi.org/10.1111/1475-6811.00008

12. Simpson, J. A. (2007). Foundations of interpersonal trust. *Social psychology: Handbook of basic principles*, *2*, 587-607.

13. And614. (2021). Together, Hands, Prayer image [Photograph]. Pixabay. https://pixabay.com/photos/together-hands-prayer-touch-5928481/

2. Rule #1: Speak Your True Self With Mindful Communication

1. Jones, S. M., & Hansen, W. (2015). The impact of mindfulness on supportive communication skills: Three exploratory studies. *Mindfulness*, *6*(5), 1115-1128. https://doi.org/10.1007/s12671-014-0362-7

2. Robins, C. J., Keng, S. L., Ekblad, A. G., & Brantley, J. G. (2012). Effects of mindfulness-based stress reduction on emotional experience and expression: A randomized controlled trial. *Journal of Clinical Psychology*, *68*(1), 117-131. https://doi.org/10.1002/jclp.20857

3. National Center for Complementary and Integrative Health. (n.d). *Meditation and mindfulness: What you need to know*. National Institutes of Health. Retrieved March 1, 2024 from https://www.nccih.nih.gov/health/meditation-and-mindfulness-what-you-need-to-know

4. Van Gordon, W., Shonin, E., & Richardson, M. (2018). Mindfulness and nature. *Mindfulness*, *9*(5), 1655-1658. https://doi.org/10.1007/s12671-018-0883-6

5. ToNic-Pics. (2016). *Leisure time, Leisure activities, Dog photography* [Photograph]. Pixabay. https://pixabay.com/photos/leisure-time-leisure-activities-1551705/

6. Khalifian, C. E., & Barry, R. A. (2020). Expanding intimacy theory: Vulnerable disclosures and partner responding. *Journal of*

Social and Personal Relationships, 37(1), 58-76. https://doi.org/10.1177/0265407519853047

7. Greyerbaby. (2014). *Hands, Words, Meaning* [Photograph]. Pixabay. https://pixabay.com/photos/hands-words-meaning-fingers-423794/

8. Richards, J. M., & Gross, J. J. (1999). Composure at any cost? The cognitive consequences of emotion suppression. *Personality and Social Psychology Bulletin, 25*(8), 1033-1044. https://doi.org/10.1177/01461672992511010

9. Guy-Evans, O. (2023). Primary and secondary emotions: Recognizing the difference. *Simply Scholar*. Retrieved March 1, 2024 from https://www.simplypsychology.org/primary-and-secondary-emotions.html

3. Rule #2: Use The Power Of Self-Awareness

1. Nabokov, V. (1990). Strong opinions. Vintage.

2. Rochat, P. (2003). Five levels of self-awareness as they unfold early in life. *Consciousness and Cognition, 12*(4), 717-731. https://doi.org/10.1016/S1053-8100(03)00081-3

3. Sutton, A. (2016). Measuring the effects of self-awareness: Construction of the self-awareness outcomes questionnaire. *Europe's Journal of Psychology, 12*(4), 645. https://doi.org/10.5964/ejop.v12i4.1178

4. Kanesan, P., & Fauzan, N. (2019). Models of emotional intelligence: A review. *e-BANGI Journal, suppl. Special Issue 7*(16), 1-9. Retrieved from https://ejournal.ukm.my/ebangi/article/view/34511

5. Thorndike, E. L. (1920). Intelligence and its uses. *Harper's Magazine, 140*, 227–235. Retrieved from https://harpers.org/archive/1920/01/intelligence-and-its-uses/

6. Salovey, P., & Mayer, J. D. (1990). Emotional Intelligence. *Imagination., Cognition and Personality, 9*(3), 185-211. https://doi.org/10.2190/DUGG-P24E-52WK-6CDG

7. Von Scheve, C. (2012). Emotion regulation and emotion work: Two sides of the same coin?. *Frontiers in Psychology, 3*, 32362. https://doi.org/10.3389/fpsyg.2012.00496

8. Varnum, M. E. (2019). Social norms are becoming weaker. *Nature Human Behaviour, 3*(3), 211-211. https://doi.org/10.1038/s41562-018-0519-9

9. Ardelt, M., & Grunwald, S. (2018). The importance of self-reflection and awareness for human development in hard times.

Research in Human Development, 15(3-4), 187-199. https://doi.org/10.1080/15427609.2018.1489098

10. Johnhain. (2015). *Mindset Mindfulness Meditation royalty-free stock* [Illustration]. Pixabay. https://pixabay.com/illustrations/mindset-mindfulness-meditation-743161/

11. Degner, J., & Wentura, D. (2010). Automatic prejudice in childhood and early adolescence. *Journal of Personality and Social Psychology, 98*(3), 356. https://doi.org/10.1037/a0017993

12. Kleka, P., Brycz, H., Fanslau, A., & Pilarska, A. (2019). Becoming aware of one's own biases in emerging adulthood—A longitudinal study. Metacognitive approach. *Advances in Cognitive Psychology, 15*(4), 308. https://doi.org/10.5709/acp-0278-y

13. Crandall, C. S., Bahns, A. J., Warner, R., & Schaller, M. (2011). Stereotypes as justifications of prejudice. *Personality and Social Psychology Bulletin, 37*(11), 1488-1498. https://doi.org/10.1177/0146167211411723

14. Lemay, E. P., Jr., Cutri, J., & Teneva, N. (2024). How loneliness undermines close relationships and persists over time: The role of perceived regard and care. *Journal of Personality and Social Psychology. Advance online publication.* https://doi.org/10.1037/pspi0000451

15. Phillipneho. (2017). *Father and son, Father, Son* [Photograph]. Pixabay. https://pixabay.com/photos/father-and-son-father-son-2695671/

4. Rule #3: Don't Just Hear—But Listen!

1. (2016). *Man, Thoughtful, Afghan* [Photograph]. Pixabay. https://pixabay.com/photos/man-thoughtful-afghan-listening-1574124/

2. Gordon, T. (2008). *Parent effectiveness training: The proven program for raising responsible children.* Harmony.

3. Cowling, C., & Van Gordon, W. (2022). Mindful parenting: Future directions and challenges. International Journal of Spa and Wellness, 5(1), 50-70. https://doi.org/10.1080/24721735.2021.1961114

4. Jones, S. M., Bodie, G. D., & Hughes, S. D. (2019). The impact of mindfulness on empathy, active listening, and perceived provisions of emotional support. *Communication Research, 46*(6), 838-865. https://doi.org/10.1177/0093650215626983

5. Ananian. (2014). *Two young people demonstrating a lively conversation* [Photograph]. Wikimedia Commons. https://commons.wikimedia.org/wiki/File:Two_young_people_demonstrating_a_lively_conversation.jpg

6. Weger Jr, H., Castle Bell, G., Minei, E. M., & Robinson, M. C. (2014). The relative effectiveness of active listening in initial interactions. *International Journal of Listening, 28*(1), 13-31. https://doi.org/10.1080/10904018.2013.813234

7. Brownell, J. (2010). The skills of listening-centered communication. In *Listening and human communication in the 21st century*, 141-157. https://doi.org/10.1002/9781444314908.ch6

8. Topornycky, J., & Golparian, S. (2016). Balancing openness and interpretation in active listening. *Collected Essays on Learning and Teaching, 9*, 175-184. https://doi.org/10.22329/celt.v9i0.4430

9. Surprising_SnapShots. (2024). *People, Couple, Conversation* [Photograph]. Pixabay. https://pixabay.com/photos/people-couple-conversation-talking-8550642/

10. Baer, R. A., Smith, G. T., Lykins, E., Button, D., Krietemeyer, J., Sauer, S., & et. al. (2008). Construct validity of the five facet mindfulness questionnaire in meditating and nonmeditating samples. *Assessment, 15*(3)

11. Bauer, C., Figl, K., & Motschnig-Pitrik, R. (2010). Introducing 'active listening' to instant messaging and e-mail: Benefits and limitations. *IADIS International Journal on WWW/Internet, 7*(2), 1-17.

5. Rule #4: All About Empathy And Cultural Intelligence

1. Aririguzoh, S. (2022). Communication competencies, culture and SDGs: Effective processes to cross-cultural communication. *Humanities and Social Sciences Communications, 9*(1), 1-11. https://doi.org/10.1057/s41599-022-01109-4

2. Earley, P. C., & Mosakowski, E. (2004). Cultural intelligence. *Harvard Business Review, 82*(10), 139-146. Retrieved from https://hbr.org/2004/10/cultural-intelligence

3. Merkin, R., Taras, V., & Steel, P. (2014). State of the art themes in cross-cultural communication research: A systematic and meta-analytic review. *International Journal of Intercultural Relations, 38*, 1-23. https://doi.org/10.1016/j.ijintrel.2013.10.004

4. Cuevas, J. A. (2022). The authoritarian threat to public education: Attacks on diversity, equity, and inclusion undermine teaching and learning. *Journal of Language and Literacy Education, 18*(2), 1-6. Retrieved from http://jolle.coe.uga.edu/wp-content/uploads/2022/12/Cuevas-2022-Final.pdf

5. Cash, T. A., Gueci, N., & Pipe, T. (2021). Equitable mindfulness: A framework for transformative conversations in higher education.

Building Healthy Academic Communities Journal, 5(1), 9-21. https://doi. org/10.18061/bhac.v5i1.7770

6. Eisenberg, J., Lee, H. J., Brück, F., Brenner, B., Claes, M. T., Mironski, J., & Bell, R. (2013). Can business schools make students culturally competent? Effects of cross-cultural management courses on cultural intelligence. *Academy of Management Learning & Education, 12*(4), 603-621. https://doi.org/10.5465/amle.2012.0022

7. Geralt. (2017). Exhibition, Visitors, Gallery image [Photograph]. Pixabay. https://pixabay.com/photos/exhibition-visitors-gallery-viewer-2944064/

8. McLaren, L. M. (2012). The cultural divide in Europe: Migration, multiculturalism, and political trust. *World Politics, 64*(2), 199-241. https://doi.org/10.1017/S0043887112000032

9.

6. Rule #5: Don't Be Afraid To Face Conflicts!

1. Mayer, B. S. (2010). *The dynamics of conflict resolution: A practitioner's guide.* John Wiley & Sons.

2. Adejimola, A. S. (2009). Language and communication in conflict resolution. *Journal of Law and Conflict Resolution, 1*(1), 001-009. Retrieved from https://academicjournals.org/article/article1379322393_Adejimola.pdf

3. Brewer, M. B. (2011). Identity and conflict. In D. Bar-Tal (Ed.), *Intergroup conflicts and their resolution: A social psychological perspective* (pp. 125–143). Psychology Press.

4. Canary, D. J. (2003). Managing interpersonal conflict: A model of events related to strategic choices. In *Handbook of communication and social interaction skills* (pp. 533-568). Routledge.

5. De Raeve, L., Jansen, N. W., van den Brandt, P. A., Vasse, R. M., & Kant, I. (2008). Risk factors for interpersonal conflicts at work. *Scandinavian Journal of Work, Environment & Health, 34*(2), 96-106. https://doi.org/10.5271/sjweh.1223

6. Nguyen, T. P., Karney, B. R., & Bradbury, T. N. (2020). When poor communication does and does not matter: The moderating role of stress. Journal of Family Psychology, 34(6), 676. https://doi.org/10.1037/fam0000643

7. National Collaborating Centre for Mental Health. (2015). *Violence and aggression: Short-term management in mental health, health and community settings.* British Psychological Society.

8. Spielfogel, J. E., & McMillen, J. C. (2017). Current use of de-escalation strategies: Similarities and differences in de-escalation

across professions. *Social Work in Mental Health, 15*(3), 232-248. https://doi.org/10.1080/15332985.2016.1212774

9. Chambers, J. R., & De Dreu, C. K. (2014). Egocentrism drives misunderstanding in conflict and negotiation. *Journal of Experimental Social Psychology, 51,* 15-26. https://doi.org/10.1016/j.jesp.2013.11.001

10. stevepb. (2014). Egg, Hammer, Hit [Photograph]. Pixabay. https://pixabay.com/photos/egg-hammer-hit-beat-fragile-583163/

11. Nair, N. (2008). Towards understanding the role of emotions in conflict: A review and future directions. *International Journal of Conflict Management, 19*(4), 359-381. https://doi.org/10.1108/10444060810909301

12. Rosenberg, M. B., & Chopra, D. (2015). *Nonviolent communication: A language of life: Life-changing tools for healthy relationships.* PuddleDancer Press.

13. Furman, F. K. (2010). Compassionate listening as a path to conflict resolution. *Journal for the Study of Peace and Conflict,* 24-38. Retrieve from https://www.proquest.com/openview/a9705377d17538c5fd42ff640d721b3d/1?pq-origsite=gscholar&cbl=506343

14. Kaufman, S., Elliott, M., & Shmueli, D. (2003). Frames, framing and reframing. In Burgess, G. & Burgess, H. (Eds). *Beyond Intractability.* Conflict Information Consortium, University of Colorado, Boulder. Retrieved from https://www.beyondintractability.org/essay/framing

15. johnhain. (2014). Conflict Disagreement Discussion royalty-free stock [Illustration]. Pixabay. https://pixabay.com/illustrations/conflict-disagreement-discussion-405744/

16. Van Dorn, R., Volavka, J., & Johnson, N. (2012). Mental disorder and violence: Is there a relationship beyond substance use?. *Social Psychiatry and Psychiatric Epidemiology, 47*(3), 487-503. https://doi.org/10.1007/s00127-011-0356-x

17. Rueve M.E., & Welton R.S. (2008).Violence and mental illness. *Psychiatry (Edgmont), 5*(5), 34-48. Retrieved from https://pubmed.ncbi.nlm.nih.gov/19727251/

18. Ronningstam, E. (2010). Narcissistic personality disorder: A current review. Current Psychiatry Reports, 12, 68-75. https://doi.org/10.1007/s11920-009-0084-z

7. Why Talking To Yourself Is NOT A Bad Thing

1. Heavey, C. L., & Hurlburt, R. T. (2008). The phenomena of inner experience. *Consciousness and cognition, 17*(3), 798-810. https://doi.org/10.1016/j.concog.2007.12.006

2. Leary, M. R., & Tangney, J. P. (2003). The self as an organizing construct in the behavioral and social sciences. In M. R. Leary & J. P. Tangney (Eds.), *Handbook of self and identity* (2nd ed., pp. 1–18). The Guilford Press.

3. Morin, A. (2005). Possible links between self-awareness and inner speech: Theoretical background, underlying mechanisms, and empirical evidence. *Journal of Consciousness Studies, 12*(4-5), 115-134.

4. Oleś, P. K., Brinthaupt, T. M., Dier, R., & Polak, D. (2020). Types of inner dialogues and functions of self-talk: Comparisons and implications. *Frontiers in Psychology*, 11, 486136. https://doi.org/10.3389/fpsyg.2020.00227

5. Mori, M., & Tanno, Y. (2015). Mediating role of decentering in the associations between self-reflection, self-rumination, and depressive symptoms. *Psychology, 6*(5), 613-621. https://doi.org/10.4236/psych.2015.65059

6. silviarita. (2019). Web, Boardwalk, Water [Photograph]. Pixabay. https://pixabay.com/photos/web-boardwalk-water-pond-4642723/

7. Leontiev, D., & Salikhova, A. (2010). Looking at oneself as inner dialogue. *International Journal for Dialogical Science, 4*(2), 95-104. Retrieved from https://ijds.lemoyne.edu/journal/4_2/pdf/IJDS.4.2.06.Leontiev-Salikhova.pdf

8. Racy, F., & Morin, A. (2024). Relationships between self-talk, inner speech, mind wandering, mindfulness, self-concept clarity, and self-regulation in university students. *Behavioral Sciences, 14*(1), 55. https://doi.org/10.3390/bs14010055

9. Baer, R. A., Smith, G. T., Hopkins, J., Krietemeyer, J., & Toney, L. (2006). Using self-report assessment methods to explore facets of mindfulness. *Assessment, 13*(1), 27-45. https://doi.org/10.1177/1073191105283504

10. Kingman, Alex. (n.d.) *How well do you know yourself? The question game.* Retrieved April 10, 2024 from https://alexkingman.com/2017/09/04/how-well-do-you-know-yourself-the-question-game/

11. Hensley, L. C., & Munn, K. J. (2020). The power of writing about procrastination: Journaling as a tool for change. *Journal of Further*

and Higher Education, 44(10), 1450-1465. https://doi.org/10.1080/0309877X.2019.1702154

12. Ackerman, C., & Millacci, T. (n.d.) *87 self-reflection questions for introspection [+Exercises]*. Positive Psychology. Retrieved April 10, 2024 from https://positivepsychology.com/introspection-self-reflection/

13. Rayple, C. & Johnson, J. (n.d.) *Ready, set, journal! 64 Journaling prompts for self-discovery*. Psychcentral. Retrieved April 10, 2024 from https://psychcentral.com/blog/ready-set-journal-64-journaling-prompts-for-self-discovery

14. PickMeUpPoetry. (n.d.) *11+ poems about self introspection: Uncovering the real you*. Retrieved April 10, 2024 from https://pickmeuppoetry.org/10-poems-about-self-introspection/

15. Masterclass. (n.d.) 11 rules for writing good poetry. Retrieved April 10, 2024 from https://www.masterclass.com/articles/how-to-write-poetry

16. Smiley, H.K. (2024, February 6) How to start writing poetry (For beginners). Wallflower Journal. Retrieved April 10, 2024 from https://www.wallflowerjournal.com/lifestyle/how-to-start-writing-poetry-for-beginners

17. Pandey, R., Tiwari, G. K., & Rai, P. K. (2020). "Bouncing back" with self-affirmation intervention: A case of Indian adults with depressive tendencies. *Madhya Bharti, 79*(2), 252-263.

18. Mindtools.com. (n.d.) *Using Affirmations*. Retrieved April 10, 2024 from https://www.mindtools.com/air49f4/using-affirmations

19. Diefenbach, S., & Borrmann, K. (2019, May). The smartphone as a pacifier and its consequences: Young adults' smartphone usage in moments of solitude and correlations to self-reflection. In *Proceedings of the 2019 CHI Conference on Human Factors in Computing Systems* (pp. 1-14). https://doi.org/10.1145/3290605.3300536

20. Pexels. (2016). *Adult, Diary, Journal* [Photograph]. Pixabay. https://pixabay.com/photos/adult-diary-journal-notebook-book-1850177/

8. Nurturing Relationships IRL

1. Schoebi, D., & Randall, A. K. (2015). Emotional dynamics in intimate relationships. *Emotion Review, 7*(4), 342-348. https://doi.org/10.1177/1754073915590620

2. Sels, L., Ceulemans, E., Bulteel, K., & Kuppens, P. (2016). Emotional interdependence and well-being in close relationships. *Frontiers in Psychology*, 7, 175470. https://doi.org/10.3389/fpsyg.2016.00283

3. Mikulincer, M., & Shaver, P. R. (2005). Attachment theory and emotions in close relationships: Exploring the attachment-related dynamics of emotional reactions to relational events. *Personal Relationships*, *12*(2), 149-168. https://doi.org/10.1111/j.1350-4126.2005.00108.x

4. Wachs, K., & Cordova, J. V. (2007). Mindful relating: Exploring mindfulness and emotion repertoires in intimate relationships. *Journal of Marital and Family Therapy*, *33*(4), 464-481. https://doi.org/10.1111/j.1752-0606.2007.00032.x

5. MabelAmber. (2018). Person, Woman, Together [Photograph]. Pixabay. https://pixabay.com/photos/person-woman-together-two-women-3382248/

6. Huinink, J., Brüderl, J., Nauck, B., Walper, S., Castiglioni, L., & Feldhaus, M. (2011). Panel analysis of intimate relationships and family dynamics (pairfam): Conceptual framework and design. *Zeitschrift für Familienforschung*, *23*(1), 77-101. https://doi.org/10.20377/jfr-235

7. Pixabay. (2016). People, Talking, Men [Photograph]. https://pixabay.com/photos/people-talking-men-male-1164926/

8. Duncan, L. G., Coatsworth, J. D., & Greenberg, M. T. (2009). A model of mindful parenting: Implications for parent–child relationships and prevention research. *Clinical Child and Family Psychology review*, *12*(3), 255-270. https://doi.org/10.1007/s10567-009-0046-3

9. Bögels, S. M., Lehtonen, A., & Restifo, K. (2010). Mindful parenting in mental health care. *Mindfulness*, *1*(2), 107-120. https://doi.org/10.1007/s12671-010-0014-5

10. Doinita, N. E., & Maria, N. D. (2015). Attachment and parenting styles. *Procedia-Social and Behavioral Sciences*, 203, 199-204. https://doi.org/10.1016/j.sbspro.2015.08.282

11. Ahemaitijiang, N., Fang, H., Ren, Y., Han, Z. R., & Singh, N. N. (2021). A review of mindful parenting: Theory, measurement, correlates, and outcomes. *Journal of Pacific Rim Psychology*, 15, 1-20. https://doi.org/10.1177/18344909211037016

12. Overall, N. C., & McNulty, J. K. (2017). What type of communication during conflict is beneficial for intimate relationships?. *Current Opinion in Psychology*, 13, 1-5. https://doi.org/doi:10.1016/j.copsyc.2016.03.002

9. Let's Make It Work At Work!

1. Pryce-Jones, J. (2010). *Happiness at work: Maximizing your psychological capital for success.* Wiley Blackwell. https://doi.org/10.1002/9780470666845

2. Fuller, M., Kamans, E., van Vuuren, M., Wolfensberger, M., & de Jong, M. D. (2021). Conceptualizing empathy competence: A professional communication perspective. *Journal of Business and Technical Communication, 35*(3), 333-368. https://doi.org/10.1177/10506519211001125

3. Wepfer, A. G., Allen, T. D., Brauchli, R., Jenny, G. J., & Bauer, G. F. (2018). Work-life boundaries and well-being: Does work-to-life integration impair well-being through lack of recovery?. *Journal of Business and Psychology, 33*(1), 727-740. https://doi.org/10.1007/s10869-017-9520-y

4. Anrita1705. (2020). Work life balance, Hd wallpaper, Work [Photograph]. Pixabay. https://pixabay.com/photos/work-life-balance-work-nature-5333786/

5. Dumbravă, G. (2011). Workplace relations and emotional intelligence. *Annals of the University of Petroşani. Economics, 11*(3), 85-92. Retrieved from https://www.upet.ro/annals/economics/pdf/2011/part3/Dumbrava.pdf

6. Brewer, E. C., & Holmes, T. L. (2016). Better communication=better teams: A communication exercise to improve team performance. In *IEEE Transactions on Professional Communication, 59*(3), 288-298. https://doi.org/10.1109/TPC.2016.2590018

7. StockSnap. (2017). People, Girls, Women [Photograph]. Pixabay. https://pixabay.com/photos/people-girls-women-students-2557396/

8. Raappana, M., & Horila, T. (2020). Team communication in the workplace. In L. Mikkola, & M. Valo (Eds.), *Workplace Communication* (pp. 28-40). Routledge. https://doi.org/10.4324/9780429196881-3

9. Oviawe, E. D. O. S. A. (2015). *Delegation: Benefits, Limitations & Why Managers Find It Difficult To Delegate.* Paper Presentation at the Nasarawa State University, Nigeria. Retrieved from https://www.academia.edu/10017316/Delegation_Benefits_Limitations_and_Why_Managers_Find_It_Difficult_To_Delegate

10. Mathebula, B., & Barnard, B. (2020). The factors of delegation success: accountability, compliance and work quality. *Expert Journal*

of Business and Management, 8(1), 76-97. Retrieved from https://business.expertjournals.com/23446781-805/

11. Soltani, M., Al-Taha, H., Mirhusseini, M., & MORTAZAVI, F. (2015). The impact of conflict in workplace on job burnout by considering the role of organizational climate. *International Journal of Modern Management and Foresight, 2*(1), 1-11.

12. Myers-Briggs Company. (2022). *Conflict at work: A research report.* Retrieved April 16, 2024 from https://www.themyersbriggs.com/en-US/Programs/Conflict-at-Work-Research

13. Lim, J. H., & Yazdanifard, R. (2012). The difference of conflict management styles and conflict resolution in workplace. *Business & Entrepreneurship Journal, 1*(1), 141-155. Retrieved from https://www.scienpress.com/Upload/BEJ/Vol%201_1_9.pdf

14. Moss, S. E., & Sanchez, J. I. (2004). Are your employees avoiding you? Managerial strategies for closing the feedback gap. *Academy of Management Perspectives, 18*(1), 32-44. Retrieved from https://web.archive.org/web/20160909134925id_/http://ww2.valdosta.edu:80/~mschnake/MossSanchez2004.pdf

10. Turn Strangers Into Meaningful Connections

1. Van Lange, P. A., & Columbus, S. (2021). Vitamin S: Why is social contact, even with strangers, so important to well-being?. *Current Directions in Psychological Science, 30*(3), 267-273. https://doi.org/10.1177/09637214211002538

2. Atir, S., Zhao, X., & Echelbarger, M. (2023). Talking to strangers: Intention, competence, and opportunity. *Current Opinion in Psychology,* 51, 101588. https://doi.org/10.1016/j.copsyc.2023.101588

3. Jeste, D. V., Lee, E. E., & Cacioppo, S. (2020). Battling the modern behavioral epidemic of loneliness: suggestions for research and interventions. *JAMA Psychiatry, 77*(6), 553-554. https://doi.org/10.1001/jamapsychiatry.2020.0027

4. Epley, N., & Schroeder, J. (2014). Mistakenly seeking solitude. *Journal of Experimental Psychology: General, 143*(5), 1980-1999. https://doi.org/10.1037/a0037323

5. Heeren, A., & McNally, R. J. (2018). Social anxiety disorder as a densely interconnected network of fear and avoidance for social situations. *Cognitive Therapy and Research, 42*(1), 503-113. https://doi.org/10.1007/s10608-017-9876-3

6. National Institute of Mental Health. (2024). Social Anxiety Disorder. Retrieved April 17, 2024 from https://www.nimh.nih.gov/health/statistics/social-anxiety-disorder

7. Twg_theworldgrad. (2023). People, Friends, Students [Photograph]. Pixabay. https://pixabay.com/photos/people-friends-students-8176890/

8. Davis, J., Wolff, H. G., Forret, M. L., & Sullivan, S. E. (2020). Networking via LinkedIn: An examination of usage and career benefits. *Journal of Vocational Behavior*, 118, 103396. https://doi.org/10.1016/j.jvb.2020.103396

9. Zhang, Y., & Leung, L. (2015). A review of social networking service (SNS) research in communication journals from 2006 to 2011. *New Media & Society*, *17*(7), 1007-1024. https://doi.org/10.1177/1461444813520477

10. Cozendo. (2016). Coffee break, Conference, Women [Photograph]. Pixabay. https://pixabay.com/photos/coffee-break-conference-women-1177540/

11. The Talk That Changes The World

1. Strand, G. (nd). *The crying Indian*. Orion Magazine. Retrieved April 24, 2024 from https://orionmagazine.org/article/the-crying-indian/

2. Tilly, C., & Wood, L. J. (2015). *Social movements, 1768-2012*. Routledge.

3. McAnany, E. G. (2012). *Saving the world: A brief history of communication for development and social change*. University of Illinois Press.

4. Robinson, K. (2018, July 13). *#METOO: Examining Communication Toward Meaningful Change*. Institute for Public Relations. Retrieved from https://instituteforpr.org/metoo-examining-employee-organization-relationships-organizational-culture-and-transparent-communication-toward-meaningful-change/

5. United Nations Sustainable Development Group. (2022, June). *Guidelines for Communications and Advocacy Strategy for the Cooperation Framework*. Retrieved from https://unsdg.un.org/resources/guidelines-communications-and-advocacy-strategy-cooperation-framework

6. Muhammed T, S., & Mathew, S. K. (2022). The disaster of misinformation: A review of research in social media. *International Journal of Data Science and Analytics*, *13*(4), 271-285. https://doi.org/10.1155/2022/8445890

7. Bick, R., Halsey, E., & Ekenga, C. C. (2018). The global environmental injustice of fast fashion. *Environmental Health, 17*(92), 1-4. https://doi.org/10.1186/s12940-018-0433-7

8. Mustafa, S., Jamil, K., Zhang, L., & Girmay, M. B. (2022). Does public awareness matter to achieve the UN's Sustainable Development Goal 6: Clean Water for Everyone?. *Journal of Environmental and Public Health.* https://doi.org/10.1155/2022/8445890

9. Wilkins, K. G. (2014). Advocacy communication. In Wilkins, K.G. & et. al. (Eds.). *The handbook of development communication and social change,* 57-71. Wiley Publishers.

10. ALS Organization. *ALS Ice Bucket Challenge:10th Anniversary.* Retrieved April 27, 2024 from https://www.als.org/IBC

11. RyanMcGuire. (2014). Woman, Splash, Water [Photograph]. Pixabay. https://pixabay.com/photos/woman-splash-water-face-glasses-438399/

12. Viray, S., & Nash, R. J. (2014). Taming the madvocate within: Social justice meets social compassion. *About Campus, 19*(5), 20-27. https://doi.org/10.1002/abc.21170

13. Bargh, J. A., & McKenna, K. Y. (2004). The Internet and social life. *Annual Review of Psychology, 55*, 573-590. https://doi.org/10.1146/annurev.psych.55.090902.141922

14. Pew Research Center. (January 31, 2024). *Social Media Fact Sheet.* Retrieved from https://www.pewresearch.org/internet/fact-sheet/social-media/

15. Kidd, D., & McIntosh, K. (2016). Social media and social movements. *Sociology Compass, 10*(9), 785-794. https://doi.org/10.1111/soc4.12399

16. Centers for Disease Control. (2024, February 5). *Tips, impact, and results.* Retrieved from https://www.cdc.gov/tobacco/campaign/tips/about/impact/campaign-impact-results.html

17. Trend Watching. (2021, August 24). *Innovation of the day: Ocean bottle.* Retrieved from https://www.trendwatching.com/innovation-of-the-day/ocean-bottle-eco-confessions

18. WebTechExperts. (2020). Social media, Social, Marketing [Illustration]. Pixabay. https://pixabay.com/illustrations/social-media-social-marketing-5187243/

19. Kent, M. L., & Taylor, M. (2021). Fostering dialogic engagement: Toward an architecture of social media for social change. *Social Media+ Society, 7*(1). https://doi.org/10.1177/2056305120984462

DISCLAIMER

The information contained in this book and its components, is meant to serve as a comprehensive collection of strategies that the author of this book has done research about. Summaries, strategies, tips and tricks are only recommendations by the author, and reading this book will not guarantee that one's results will exactly mirror the author's results.

The author of this book has made all reasonable efforts to provide current and accurate information for the readers of this book. The author and their associates will not be held liable for any unintentional errors or omissions that may be found, and for damages arising from the use or misuse of the information presented in this book.

Readers should exercise their own judgment and discretion in interpreting and applying the information to their specific circumstances. This book is not intended to replace professional advice (especially medical advice, diagnosis, or treatment). Readers are encouraged to seek appropriate professional guidance for their individual needs.

The material in the book may include information by third parties. Third party materials comprise of opinions expressed by their owners. As such, the author of this book does not assume responsibility or liability for any third party material or opinions.

The publication of third party material does not constitute the author's guarantee of any information, products, services, or opinions contained within third party material. Use of third party material does not guarantee that your results will mirror our results. Publication of such third party material is simply a recommendation and expression of the author's own opinion of that material.

Whether because of the progression of the Internet, or the unforeseen changes in company policy and editorial submission guidelines, what is stated as fact at the time of this writing may become outdated or inapplicable later.

Social IQ Academy is committed to respecting copyright laws and intellectual property rights. We have taken reasonable measures to ensure that all quotes, diagrams, figures, images, tables, and other information used in this publication are either created by us, obtained with permission, or fall under fair use guidelines. However, if any copyright infringement has inadvertently occurred, please notify us promptly, providing sufficient details to identify the specific material in question. We will take immediate action to rectify the situation, which may include obtaining necessary permissions, making corrections, or removing the material in subsequent editions or reprints.

Made in the USA
Coppell, TX
25 August 2024

36426691R00156